The

Gettysburg

What Was It Like For the Citizens of 1863?

By

Linda Clark

Thanks 4 Reading!

Linda Clark

View the Battle of Gettysburg and its aftermath through the eyes of an array of real local civilians who witnessed this human tragedy of catastrophic proportion. Relive the trauma and fear endured by citizens, young and old, as they hovered in their cellars while the world around them changed forever.

The

Battle

What Was It Like **FOR** the Citizens of 1863?

Gettysburg

Copyright 2012 by Linda Clark

ISBN - 978-0-9853899-0-1

For additional copies contact pausetoread@yahoo.com or visit the
website www.pausetoreadbooks.webs.com

First printing – Printed in the U.S.A

Second printing with additions – 2013 – Printed in the U.S. A.

&Dedication

This book is dedicated to my parents, Charles and Arlene (Epley) Heintzelman, who took me to many historical events in Gettysburg throughout my childhood, and to my husband, David, who encourages me in my historical endeavors. Thank you!

This book was created to honor the memory of the real people mentioned on these pages. May their stories inspire the future by illuminating the past.

&Acknowledgements

Sincere appreciation is extended to fellow Licensed Battlefield Guide Debra Novotny for her encouragement throughout this project, and for confirming the historical accuracy of facts and events.

Appreciation is also extended to those dedicated staff members and volunteers of the Adams County Historical Society who have offered assistance in the acquisition of primary sources used in this book. Special thanks to the following: Wayne Motts, Timothy Smith, Elwood Christ, and the late Sarah Fuss. Thanks to these contemporary Gettysburg citizens who made this book about 1863 Gettysburg citizens possible.

And thanks to you, the reader, for taking time out of your "present" to learn about real people of the past. May your reading time be well rewarded with information and inspiration. – L.M.C.

❧Table of Contents

❧Map Locations and Maps

Baltimore Street
Adams County Courthouse – 101
Fannie Buehler – 112
David Buehler – 112
Agnes Barr – 220
Matilda Pierce – 303
Georgia McClellan – 518
Elizabeth Thorn – 799

Chambersburg Street
College Lutheran Church – 30
Annie Skelly – 33
Mary McAllister – 43
Elizabeth Gilbert – 213
Sarah Broadhead -217
John Burns – 252

West Middle Street
Mary Warren – 237
Julia Jacobs – 103
Henry Jacobs – 103
Daniel Skelly – 47

York Street, Carlisle Street, Pennsylvania College
Sarah King – 165 York Street
Emma Yount – 32 Carlisle Street
Washington House – 32 Carlisle
Nellie Auchinbaugh – 104 Carlisle
Charles Schick – 125 Carlisle
T. F. Shuey- Pennsylvania College on North Washington Street

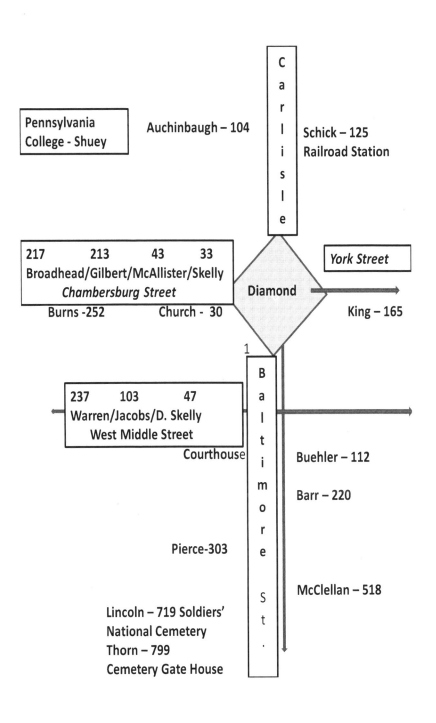

Pennsylvania College - Shuey

Auchinbaugh – 104

Carlisle

Schick – 125
Railroad Station

217   213   43   33
Broadhead/Gilbert/McAllister/Skelly
Chambersburg Street
Burns -252   Church - 30

Diamond

York Street

King – 165

1
Baltimore St.

237   103   47
Warren/Jacobs/D. Skelly
West Middle Street

Courthouse

Buehler – 112

Barr – 220

Pierce-303

McClellan – 518

Lincoln – 719 Soldiers'
National Cemetery
Thorn – 799
Cemetery Gate House

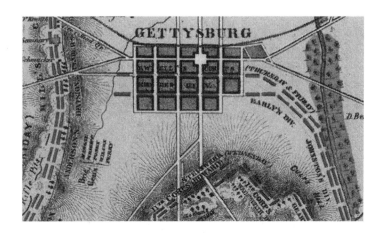

Seminary Ridge, and West and North of Town

Lydia Ziegler – Seminary Dormitory
Harriet Bayly- Newville Road
Billy Bayly- Newville Road
Amelia Harman – Mill Road
Laura McMillan – Seminary Ridge
Sadie Hoffman – Seminary Ridge

South and East of Town, and the Far West

James Tawney – Low Dutch Road
Isaac Durboraw – Baltimore Pike
David Conover – Baltimore Pike
Eliza Farnham – California!
Abraham Lincoln – Kentucky, Indiana, Illinois, Washington, D.C.

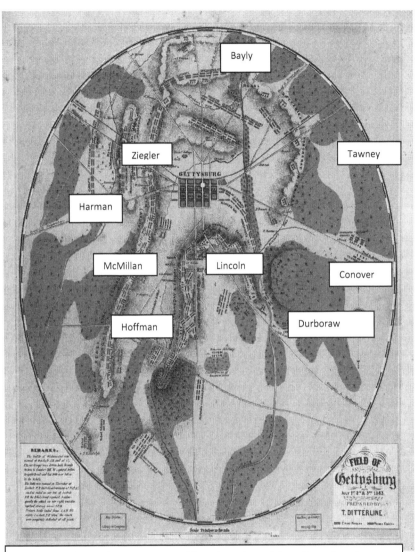

This oval-shaped map, created by Theodore Ditterline shortly after the battle, depicts troops and artillery positions along with roads, railways, and houses. Ditterline was an Adams County school teacher and art journal salesman. He is buried in the Evergreen Cemetery.

❧Introduction

During the summer of 1863 the citizens of Gettysburg were surrounded by the conflict which is still known throughout the world as the most significant battle of our American Civil War. Much has been written concerning that battle from the viewpoint of the soldiers taking part in the military action. However, many local citizens experienced the battle from their cellars and beyond. They also wrote of their struggles during that terrible summer. Some of these first-hand accounts were written as diaries, others as newspaper articles, and still others as personal letters to relatives. All contain compelling and insightful information.

These primary sources were written in the first person and were utilized as the reference material for each of the following accounts. *For this reason, the biographical sketches that follow have also been written in the first person.* The immediacy felt by the citizens is evident. Most can be proven to be historically accurate, although a few details may have become clouded over time. Some apparent errors have been corrected within the biographies (usually written inside a pair of parentheses.)

It is interesting to note how much, and how little, the citizens were aware of during the battles. The similarities and differences among the spectators' experiences are remarkable. Each was witness to their own private set of circumstances, thus shedding their own unique insight into that dreadful season of death and destruction. Through their eyes, as revealed in their writings, we become aware of a very inimitable and turbulent time in our American history.

Included in this compilation are the most unique and interesting observations and insights distilled from much longer, often tediously detailed, documents. Some of the original language was included, such as the word "fly," which in 1863 simply meant to hurry. Back then the word "car" was sufficient to imply a railroad car since there was no other type of car at the time. Great effort was made to keep the vocabulary and character of each civilian writer intact. Such colloquialisms as "down cellar" appear in the following, along with other "Pennsylvania Dutch" language dialect.

Although the citizens featured on the following pages are of various ages and backgrounds, they have one strong common bond. All of them were caught up in circumstances beyond their control. In contrast, soldiers who joined the armies, willingly or not, expected to see battle during the war. This was not the case for these civilians living north of the Mason-Dixon during the summer of 1863. As you turn the following pages imagine yourself turning back the hands of time and learn about the real citizens of Gettysburg during the actual time of the battle. Your "friends" from the past await you. May you be enriched by their insightful reflections.

This statue of Elizabeth Thorn was created by sculptor Ron Tunison and dedicated as the Civil War Women's Memorial in November of 2002. Today it stands behind the Gatehouse of the Evergreen Cemetery. Elizabeth's story and many others await you on the following pages.

~ 13 ~

Although there are photographs of some of the real citizens included in this book, images of many are unavailable. Photography was a new technology at that time. There were no photographs taken of soldiers engaged in actual battle. Likewise, there were no photographs taken of citizens at that particular time period.

Technology has indeed transformed the way we "see" the world. Photographers of the time period arrived on the scene at Gettysburg after the battle and took primitive, but revealing pictures of the aftermath and fields of battle. Imagine if modern camera crews had broadcast what was happening west of town on the first day of battle. Would the viewing public have allowed two more days, let alone two more years, of such gruesome carnage?

May the imageless mirror above allow your mind to visualize present- day people of similar age and status. Imagine how you and others you know may have reacted under similar circumstances. Afterall, the citizens of Gettysburg could hardly have predicted the global significance of local events, and how widely known their personal stories would become.

❧Baltimore Street and the Diamond

In 1863 the center of Gettysburg was referred to as "The Diamond." Four roads connected here, but they didn't actually cross here. At one time the Court House stood right in the middle of the Diamond! So, as travelers in horse-drawn carriages maneuvered from one direction to another, they formed a diamond-shaped thoroughfare around that government building. Today the Diamond is replaced by a traffic circle to accommodate motorized cars, buses, trucks, tractor trailers, and motorcycles as they pass through town. Occasionally a horse-drawn carriage ambles around the traffic circle providing tours for visitors to the area. And of course, people still walk along the current storefronts now present on the Diamond. Many of these buildings are original to 1863 and can be identified by bronze plaques.

Today the center of town is often referred to as Lincoln Square. In November of 1863 Abraham Lincoln was the houseguest of Attorney David Wills whose house still stands on the southeast quadrant of the square. The President traveled from the Wills' House to the dedication of the Soldiers' National Cemetery south of town. There he spoke to the crowd of about 15,000 spectators for merely a few minutes, but in doing so delivered his iconic Gettysburg Address.

The following 1863 citizens have in common a Baltimore Street address. They include the remembrances of one gentleman along with a collection of ladies varying in age and circumstance. Fannie Buehler's first-hand account is followed by the alarming adventures of her husband, David, the Postmaster of Gettysburg at the time. Agnes Barr's original account included some errors in recollection, which are corrected for this publication. Imagine the difficulty of knowing something as mundane as the day of the week when your very life hangs in the balance! This phenomenon of memory lapse can certainly explain the discrepancies in reports from soldiers in the field. Soldiers who took the time to write letters home were being as honest as possible in a chaotic situation.

Continuing south on Baltimore Street there is a downward slope followed by the gentle incline of Cemetery Hill. Although the last two Baltimore Street residents included in this section lived close together, they suffered through quite dissimilar circumstances. Georgia McClellan is a name not as well known as that of her sister, Jennie Wade. *Her* tragic story is told through the eyes of her sister, Georgia. Lastly, near the top of Cemetery Hill lived Elizabeth Thorn. Living in the Gatehouse at the Evergreen Cemetery, her experiences are nothing less than heroic. Indeed, she deserves the statue that now stands in her honor behind the Gate House.

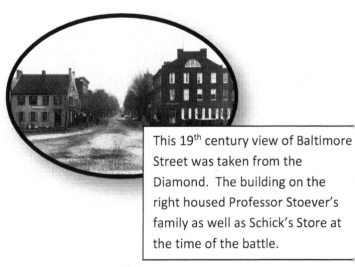

This 19th century view of Baltimore Street was taken from the Diamond. The building on the right housed Professor Stoever's family as well as Schick's Store at the time of the battle.

❖ Fannie Buehler – Wife and Mother
112 Baltimore Street

In 1863 my husband and I lived on Baltimore Street across from the new Court House. (Our old Court House had been located in the "Diamond" in the center of town). I am not writing this as a history of war or even of the battle fought here in our town. Instead, I am telling what I saw and did so that future generations may read or listen to my story while sitting around the fireplace just as I sat listening to my grandfather tell of his experiences in the American Revolutionary War.

Although my story is a sad one, I am proud to say that I was able to do at least a small part to help give our nation a new birth of freedom, as President Lincoln said. My husband was a staunch Republican. My mother, however, was a red-hot Republican, a great politician, one loyal to her flag and country. Although women of my day were not able to vote, they were still intensely patriotic. Many of us women of the North had hard times during the war, but we had great sympathy and admiration for our Sisters of the South who suffered and endured so much more. Anyway, my mother decided to take some of our children to my sister's home in New Jersey when there were rumors of the Confederate invasion into Pennsylvania.

We had been expecting a Rebel invasion for a long time. When the Rebels really came, though, they still took us unaware. On the morning of June 26th life was normal. After a very simple lunch, I went to my sewing machine to finish off a piece of work. When I heard the cry, "Mama, the Rebels are coming!" I finished my work, and then went leisurely downstairs. Upon seeing the Rebel Cavalry, I closed the shutters, locked the door, buried the keys and went to the front door with the children to watch "the Rebs" pass by. Instead of fear, I felt sympathy for these poor men in their dirty, torn garments – hatless, shoeless, and foot-sore. Since I wanted to know how long to expect them around, I sat on the front step with the children and Bruno, our faithful Newfoundland dog, to watch operations.

Confederate Generals Gordon and Early negotiated terms with our local burgess and town council. (Actually the burgess was out of town so they met with the president of the town council.) The city fathers could not grant the requisition of supplies needed, so the Confederates proposed to proceed on to York, with plans of continuing on to Philadelphia or Washington. I chatted with my neighbors, watching our new Court House and wondering if the enemy army would destroy it or perhaps destroy our entire town. Some strangers came and asked permission to sit on our steps. They chatted about how the conditions of the North were much less impoverished than their homes in the South. That night I took Bruno along to my bedroom and had him lie underneath the window. He was my only protection against a town full of Rebel soldiers.

Although these Rebel soldiers left town, Gettysburg was still the scene of a battle on July 1st. My friends urged me to fly to a safer place in the country. Since I was determined to stay, I was ordered to the cellar by officers dashing through the streets, warning us the town would be shelled. Our house had three dry cellars, so quickly I had many visitors seeking safety. Many cellars at the bottom of the Baltimore Street hill were wet from the numerous showers due to the frequent firing of guns.

Soon I was busy caring for the wounded and making bandages. When I had time I prepared our first meal. A German soldier took care of my two-year-old son Allie so I could work, while an Irishman kept the kitchen fire going and pared the vegetables. My husband had planned ahead, so our cellar was full of flour, hams, butter, eggs, coffee, sugar, tea, and apple butter. We also had a little garden with onions, peas, beans, and potatoes. During the battle Rebel soldiers searched the house including the garret and the cellar. They were looking for Union soldiers and they did not take our food supply. We took our extension table from the dining room and placed it on the porch. I think that table served food throughout the month of July. First soldiers, both friend and foe, ate there. Later Congressmen, Senators, and even Governors ate there. We charged no one for anything they ate or drank here that fearful summer.

After the battle my family was united. Friends sent us barrels and boxes of supplies to be distributed in person to the wounded. All was not happy, though. My little Allie survived the battle but died in September. He had been amused by the sounds of war. Each time a shell flew overhead he said, "Listen, Mama, do you hear the birdies?" The Death Angel came with noiseless wings and took him from our home on earth to our dear Father's home in Heaven.

Bronze plaques are now displayed on most houses that witnessed the Battle of Gettysburg in July of 1863.

❖ David Buehler – Father/Postmaster
112 Baltimore Street

My wife and I lived on Baltimore Street across from the new Court House. Since I was a lawyer, this was certainly convenient for me. Being a staunch Republican, I enjoyed editing a local Republican newspaper. Due to the war, business was depressed. Our growing family included six children, so when I was offered the position as Postmaster of our town, I gladly took it for the extra income.

Unfortunately, being a "government" official made me a marked man in the eyes of the Confederates. If the enemy captured me, I may have been sent to Libby Prison, or some other Rebel prison, and suffered to death. Much against my will, my dear wife persuaded me to prepare to leave if the enemy entered our state of Pennsylvania. I packed up a satchel with valuables, personal and official papers, and government property from my Post Office, just in case of invasion. In late June Confederates did indeed come to Gettysburg, so I fled! I grabbed the satchel, and my wife handed me an umbrella to protect me against the falling rain. I decided against the umbrella.

As I ran east on Middle Street, some Confederate cavalry was also heading east just one block away on York Street. Fortunately, that same month I had gotten a car (a train car, that is) to store our valuables in case of Rebel raiders. (Although the battle here took place in early July, we didn't get our valuables back until November.) I was the one in danger now. I hailed a horse-pulled wagon, but after the pursuing Confederates fired a few shots, I jumped from the wagon and headed for the woods.

I eventually made it to Hanover, about 15 miles away. Soaking wet and exhausted, I reached the Central Hotel on the square of that town and sent for the President of the railroad, Mr. Eichelberger. As I informed him of the burning of train cars in Gettysburg, he quickly decided to send all of his rolling stock farther east. I decided to continue on beyond York to Lancaster. It was important that I cross the Susquehanna River bridge since locals had plans to burn it to keep the Rebels from invading on to Philadelphia. It wasn't until I reached the home of my sister-in-law in Elizabeth, New Jersey, on June 29th that I read a newspaper account about the massing of troops around Gettysburg. The news about the situation grew worse and worse

On the 4th of July I was determined to return to my home despite the dangers, so anxious was I about the fate of my home and family. Although I had no trouble reaching Philadelphia, my decision on the rest of my route was uncertain. I finally made it to our state capital in Harrisburg. Although I requested a pass to return home to Gettysburg to my family, our Governor Curtin refused because he could not guarantee my safety. Totally determined to return home, I went on to York where I found a stagecoach driver who agreed to make the trip for a great sum. However, after hearing more wild reports, he decided not to risk his life and horses.

Finally I found some other gentlemen who wanted to go to Gettysburg as well and we made that driver an offer he could not refuse. Although there was evidence of great struggle, we did not see one live Rebel on our trip home. Speaking of home, I arrived there the morning of July 7th. My wife was especially surprised to see me. She had heard a report, obviously erroneous, that I had been kill

❖ Agnes Barr – 220 Baltimore Street

I was about 30 years old at the time of the Battle of Gettysburg. I lived with my mother and sister on Baltimore Street just a few doors down from the Presbyterian Church. We had recently left our farm in Mount Joy Township where my brother still lived. It was about 25 years later that I was asked to write down my remembrances of the battle, so, needless to say, some of the information may be inaccurate. I thought it was Friday the 27th when enemy soldiers arrived, but I am told it was June 26th. Although some of our neighbors decided to leave town when the Confederates arrived, my family remained.

Saturday was an anxious and sad day with no information. On the Sabbath, though, I went to the Presbyterian Church with my mother and sister. As we were returning home we saw our flag coming over the hill along with soldiers in Union dress. We were delighted to see them! (History will tell you that Buford's Union Cavalry did not arrive until June 30th, a Tuesday. Oh well!) Townspeople lined both sides of the street with their buckets of water, tin cups, and tumblers. On Tuesday morning, June 31st, more soldiers arrived. This time we were much better prepared and gave them both provisions and water. (I know what you are going to say. June only has 30 days, so obviously I really have my dates mixed up!)

On the morning of July 1st the battle really did begin and the ladies of Gettysburg were notified to prepare lint and bandages. We were out at the front door to see what was doing when a Federal officer galloped up to the church and ordered the building be opened for a hospital. That was 2:00 and soon ambulances began bringing in the wounded. Then, just past 3:00, the citizens were ordered to their cellars because the Rebels were driving our men back through the town. Mother, Margaret, and I went to the cellar and in just a short time we heard a crash at our back door in the alley. We all went upstairs and saw a Union man who was trying to get away from the Rebels. He ran out through the opposite door into the yard and hurried into the garden and we never knew what became of him.

Neighbors cared for neighbors. Mrs. Houck was sick in bed, so Alenetta, Sally Paxton and I went through houses and down the back way taking them breakfast, dinner, and supper. Bullets would whiz past us and cut the trees. One of the surgeons stopped us for coffee, and I told him to go up to my house for my mother was there and would give him coffee. Later, when I got home, I found four surgeons eating at the dinner table. And, Mother asked them to breakfast, as well!

Although we were busy all day long preparing food for the hospital, it was not safe to deliver it across the street for any reason. Confederate sharpshooters at the south end of Baltimore Street were watching for any mark to cut down. We were surrounded by Confederates! We were not really aware of the risk we were taking every time we got water from the cistern.

Again on July 2nd my family and neighbor ladies went the back way through the yards into the church to help the wounded. Boards were laid over the tops of the pews, and the wounded lay on those. By evening it was misting as we heard the shrieks and groans of more wounded out toward the cemetery. It was heart-rending! Late that evening there was a rap at the front door. A party of Confederate soldiers stood there asking for something to eat. We were just starting to the hospital with supper for the wounded and really did not have much left. At first they were defiant and rough. But when they heard we were caring for the wounded their manner changed and they said they wouldn't take from those in the hospital. Even when we told them we could give them a little bread they said no. Later that same evening Confederate soldiers on the back porch spied the blue coats of our guests. When they realized they were surgeons, they left us continue feeding them supper. When Mother offered those Confederate soldiers a plate of biscuits they refused to take them.

On July 3rd the knocker on the front door called someone, and I went to the door. Two fine looking young Confederate officers said they would like the privilege of searching our house. I told them they were welcome to do so! After going upstairs and downstairs they apologized, saying they did not doubt our word, and that it was a delicate matter, but they were compelled to do the search. Late in the afternoon we were fearful we'd run out of bread. Since the neighbors across the street had not been helping, I volunteered to go across to Dr. Runkle's house. They were frightened to see me and reminded me that I had run a great risk in crossing the street under such circumstances. They had been in their cellar all the time but had nothing prepared to give. Now, empty-handed despite my efforts, I had to get back across the street! Rebels lay at both ends of the street, screaming and laughing. As I got to my door the bullets came!

Later that night one of the surgeons said the Rebels would be leaving very soon. As Maggie and I went upstairs to bed, we saw a fire out at our stable and we supposed the Confederates were cooking our chickens. The next morning we were happy to find out that we were only partially correct. Although we did indeed find their discarded chicken bones, we also were happy to see that our chickens were still there. Also, they had access to our garden but we found nothing missing. About midnight we heard the sound of wagons and artillery. The sound continued until Saturday morning, July 4th. We reported to one of the surgeons what we heard and we then carried a flag of truce to the Federal army out at the cemetery.

After the Rebel army retreated there was quite a commotion on the streets. At about 9 or 10 o'clock a.m. Confederate General Lee sent a flag of truce and informed the citizens they should go back to their cellars because they were going to shell the town. Saturday was a full day. Soldiers continued coming to the side door and the front door wanting to buy bread. But, we had no bread to sell. We gave what we could and took no money from a private soldier. Oh, I almost forgot to tell you that we were very alarmed at the news of the shelling of the town. I am very thankful that it was not done.

We didn't even realize the next day was the Sabbath. No churches were open and our work went on as before. About noon that day the Sanitary Commission arrived as did the Christian Commission. Finally, the exhausted ladies who had been preparing food at the Presbyterian Church were relieved by these new workers Hungry soldiers still came to our doors, although our food supply was almost gone.

In the afternoon my brother Smith who lived out at the old homestead drove up to the door. His first words were, "Mother, I am so glad to see you!" He had heard reports that two women had been killed and that one of them was a Mrs. Barr. Although he had tried to get through the lines every day while the battle was going on, he couldn't get into town until Sabbath.

Soldiers continued coming to our house for food, and the surgeons continued boarding with us. Some of their names were Dr. Rullison, Dr. Sanger, Dr. Beck, Dr. Vossburg, and Dr. Butcher. Dr. Rullison wrote back to our family while he was stationed in Virginia. We were saddened to learn that he was later killed in the war. He was a pleasant gentleman and made himself very agreeable. We all felt as if we had lost a friend.

After the rush was over at the church hospital, we visited other hospitals. The school building was filled with Confederate soldiers and the Ladies of the Confederate Aristocracy took charge there. One of those ladies was actually a friend of our family before the war. We also went to visit some of the soldiers from our Presbyterian Hospital at their next location. Sister Maggie met a soldier walking with crutches because he had both legs shot off. When offered a peach, he asked that it please be placed in his mouth.

One day I went with Dr. Beck on horseback over the field. The fences were gone and the grain and corn were tramped down. The entire landscape looked like a bare road. The doctor picked up a solid shell that he found and gave it to me. I carried it home and kept it. Later in my life I opened a millinery shop on Baltimore Street.

In 1857 this new, consolidated "Union School" building was erected on High Street. It consolidated classes allowing boys and girls to be educated together. Students were replaced by wounded soldiers during and after the battle.

❖ Matilda Pierce – Teenager
303 Baltimore Street

Although my brothers James and William were already Union soldiers, I was at home when Confederate and Union forces met for battle here in my hometown of Gettysburg. My father worked as a butcher and my mother was the local manager of the Ladies Union Relief Society that helped support our boys in blue.

My life was quite ordinary for a girl of my day. I was a student at the Young Ladies' Seminary, a finishing school very near my house. It was during my Friday afternoon literary exercise that we heard the cry, "The Rebels are coming!" Mrs. Eyster, our teacher, immediately said, "Run home as quickly as you can!"

On this particular day, June 26th of 1863, the enemy army was on the march to York, a larger city closer to the Susquehanna River. What a ragged looking sight these men were! They requested much-needed supplies from local merchants but got very little. They took our horse, and then had the nerve to request food. I guess we girls showed nerve ourselves when we sang "The Union Forever" as the Rebels marched down our street.

It wasn't until June 30th that real Union troops arrived in Gettysburg. Again we sang, this time to a more appreciative crowd. These men of General Buford's Cavalry wished we knew more verses of the song. We even picked flowers for these men who came to save our town, but in our excitement, we forgot to hand them out! Then on the morning of Wednesday, July 1st we heard fighting begin west of town. All morning long our family heard the cannons roar like thunder. At about 1:00 our neighbor

Mrs. Schriver asked if I could go with her to her parent's home, the Weikert farm, south of town. It seemed to be a safer place, so my parents readily agreed. If only we could have had the ability to see into the future.

The trip to the Weikert farm was quite the adventure. Union soldiers were placing cannon right in the Evergreen Cemetery at the south edge of town. The muddy roads were so bad that we stopped at the widow Leister's house. There a soldier told us we could catch a ride on an army wagon heading in that direction. So again, we embarked on yet another adventure. The wheels sunk halfway into the mud and there were no springs!

Arriving at the Weikert farm, we saw an ammunition wagon explode, sending one man flying into the air. Little did I realize that this would be the first of many badly injured men to be cared for, victims of war. Later that day wounded soldiers began arriving from that day's battle. Some walked, some crawled, and some were carried, and they all needed something. At first I helped by pumping water. I actually served water to General Meade, the leader of the Union army. Later, when the Weikert house and barn were both filled with the suffering men, I cried. I sincerely hope that none of you will ever have to witness the terrible suffering of such brave soldiers as they lay dying.

As the battle of Gettysburg raged on for two more days, the fighting got closer. In fact, the Weikert farm was on one side of Little Round Top and heavy fighting raged on the other side. When we were told the house was no longer safe, carriages came to take us to a safer place. However, a cannon shell came hurling through the air right over my head, scaring me to death, almost. As we headed farther away from town I realized I had not eaten for some time. A kind soldier gave me a piece of his army food called hardtack. This name described the food quite well, but I ate it anyway. Besides, I had much more important things to worry about.

The earth around us shook and the cannon roared so loudly that we couldn't hear ourselves speak. It was what I saw in the distance, though, that struck the most fear in my heart. It looked like the town of Gettysburg was on fire! How I worried about my family. When I finally did return home my house and family were all safe. My own mother didn't even recognize me, though. I had to admit, I was quite a different person.

I helped army nurses as they cared for the wounded and saw amputated arms and legs piled higher than the fence. I promised a badly wounded General Weed that I would return to see him the next morning only to find him dead, yet another victim of war. I still prize a uniform button attached to a piece of gray cloth that was given to me by a Union soldier during my ordeal. It served as a reminder of a terrible event that changed my life and our country.

Tillie Pierce was at the Jacob Weikert when she met General Weed who was wounded on Little Round Top. He later died here in the cellar kitchen.

❖ Georgia McClellan –Wife/ Mother/Sister 518 Baltimore Street

I was born on the Fourth of July in 1841. So I was just 21 years old when the Battle of Gettysburg surrounded my house. I had married my husband, John Louis McClellan, on April 15 of 1862 and he soon returned to military service in the 2nd Pennsylvania Infantry regiment. Our first son was born during the summer of 1863, just one hour before Confederates marched into town on June 26th. Fortunately my mother lived nearby and was able to come and help out with the chores while I cared for young Louis Kenneth.

This made life very hard for my younger sister Mary Virginia or Jennie as she is now remembered. She was only 20 years old and had the responsibility of taking care of the family home on Breckenridge Street. In addition she was taking care of a young border, a crippled boy by the name of Isaac Brinkerhoff. The family needed the extra money this job brought in due to our father's various problems. He was arrested for keeping $300 he found, rather than trying to find the rightful owner. His larceny conviction caused him to be sentenced to two years of solitary confinement at a penitentiary.

Although Jennie also had to care for our younger brother Harry, she still found time to alter the oversized uniform of our brother Jack who enlisted in Company B of the 21ST Pennsylvania Cavalry Regiment. As if she wasn't busy enough, our twelve-year-old brother Samuel, who worked as a delivery boy for Mr. Pierce, the butcher, got captured by the Confederates and placed under arrest. When Jennie found out what happened, she came for Mother who went to the Diamond in the center of town. There

Mother spoke directly to Confederate General Jubal Early who released Sam to her.

On the morning of July 1st, as she heard the first horrible sounds of battle, Jennie took young Isaac to his home. Then she returned to the house on Breckenridge Street to get our young brother so the two of them could come and stay at my house. After all, most of the rest of the town was being held by Confederates with enemy soldiers on the streets. My house seemed safer since it was on the edge of town near the peaceful Evergreen Cemetery.

Upon arriving, poor Jennie had much work to do. Jennie supplied food and water to many Union soldiers who arrived in town preparing for battle. And she was also on hand to distribute even more water to many of those same Union troops as they were forced to retreat later that afternoon. Upon reaching the height of East Cemetery Hill, they stopped. There, on the high ground just south of my house, the Union Army prepared a defensive position against the Confederates who now held the town of Gettysburg. My little house was right between the two enemy lines! Confederate sharpshooters were actually firing in the direction of my house from second story windows of houses near my mother's house on Breckenridge Street.

Despite dead and wounded soldiers lying in our yard, Jennie went out that night with water and biscuits for the Union soldiers nearby. Perhaps she was trying to help as many soldiers as she could, knowing that she had both a brother and a brother-in-law (my husband), in uniform. Hopefully some kind women would find it in their hearts to take care of our loved ones if necessary. Although they made us feel somewhat safe, the Union soldiers on our property actually made our little brick house more of a target for the Confederate sharpshooters.

About seven o'clock on the morning of July 3rd there was so much firing at my house that the windowpanes facing the town were shattered. Earlier that morning, at about 4:30, Jennie and Sam went out back for firewood so the daily baking could be done as usual. Nothing on that particular day was usual, though. A bullet entered the house and struck the bedpost, finally landing at the foot of the bed where I was tightly holding my tiny little son.

I remember hearing Jennie say something about wishing if anyone did get hurt it should be her and not me, since I had baby Louis to care for. At about 8:30 another bullet entered the house. This one proved to change my life forever. It struck Jennie in the back, piercing her heart, as she stood kneading dough for bread. She died instantly, falling to the floor with flour still covering her fingers.

As the roar of war continued around us, our mother calmly announced, "Georgia, your sister is dead." I immediately screamed in horror, alarming the Union soldiers outside the house to our plight. They helped us down into the cellar that we reached by going down an outside staircase. The soldiers brought along a rocking chair for me. And they carried Jennie's dead body, wrapped in a quilt I had made as a girl.

We waited for 18 long hours in that dark cellar, not knowing what horrors the next minute would bring. On the afternoon of July 4th, my 22nd birthday, I stood beside my mother and two little brothers in the back yard of my home on the side of Cemetery Hill and watched my sister Jennie laid to rest.

In November of 1865, two years after President Lincoln dedicated a soldier's cemetery on Cemetery Hill, my sister Jennie was reburied in the Evergreen Cemetery, the civilian cemetery that gave its name to Cemetery Hill in the Battle of Gettysburg.

This photo, taken in 1861, shows sisters Georgia and Jennie Wade flanking a Baltimore Street neighbor, Maria Comfort. Below is the 1863 home of Georgia McClellan along with an insert of her sister, Jennie, who was killed here while baking on the morning of July 3. Jennie is the solitary citizen killed during the three day battle of Gettysburg.

❖ Elizabeth Thorn – Wife and Mother 799 Baltimore Street - Cemetery Hill

In 1855 1 married my husband Peter and we were the very first couple to live in the Gate-way House at the Evergreen Cemetery. At the time of the Battle of Gettysburg my husband was in the Union Army so I was at home with our three young boys and my parents. On the first day of fighting I remember soldiers eating the bread I baked as fast as I could cut it. I pumped so much water that the pump broke! Every vessel in the house was used by the thirsty men! As the battle began we went to the cellar. Later I heard that a guide was needed to show the commanders the location of the roads into Gettysburg. They wanted a man for the job, but my father was quite elderly and my sons quite young. So, I became the guide.

Although we spent most of the time in the cellar for safety reasons, sometimes I did go upstairs to check out our situation. A cannon shell entered the garret room where I had just been working and frightened me back downstairs. One night I made supper for three Union generals, Howard, Slocum, and Sickles. We had two dough cakes, three pieces of meat, apple butter and coffee.

Later we were told it would be safer if we left the house, and we should take only our "good" things. Of course, we thought that was everything! When we returned home several days later, everything we left behind was gone except three feather beds and a couple of pillows. These had been used for the wounded soldiers and were not fit for further use.

The following weeks were awful ones. Almost 20 men and over 30 horses had been buried in our yard. The stench was so awful 1 could hardly eat. I wore the same dress for the next six weeks for it was all that I had. That was certainly not the worst of the situation. My elderly father and I dug 105 graves for soldiers in the next three weeks. For all of this extra work I received only the regular salary of $13 a month. During the years to follow, Union General Howard continued to visit the house where he ate a midnight supper on the night of July 1, 1863.

Peter and Elizabeth Thorn became the first residents of the Gate House when Peter assumed the position of superintendent for this new private cemetery created on Raffensberger Hill south of Gettysburg. Peter joined Co. B, 138th Pennsylvania Infantry, leaving Elizabeth in charge of the cemetery. She served as caretaker from 1862-1865.

&Chambersburg Street

Chambersburg Street extends west of the Diamond and was a major route for travelers as they continued toward the frontier. The town of Chambersburg was about 25 miles away, the approximate distance a horse-pulled wagon could travel in one day. That time may have been lengthened by the rolling but rugged South Mountains, an extension of the Blue Ridge. These lovely geographic features created a complicated obstruction for travelers. Likewise, they created a natural protective partition for the Confederate Army as it invaded into the Union state of Pennsylvania. Thus, the Confederate Army of Northern Virginia marched northward up the Shenandoah Valley to invade Pennsylvania, using these mountains as a screen from the Union Army of the Potomac which was on the eastern side. As a result, most of the Rebel Army arrived in Gettysburg from the west.

The residents living on Chambersburg Street in 1863 were among the first citizens to be aware of the enemy soldiers, even before they arrived in Gettysburg the morning of July 1st. Ominously, the mountain campfires of these Rebels were visible from the town even the night before. Imagine how important this information was to these citizens who lived in a world without the vast array of technological advances we enjoy today. Although there were several newspapers published in Gettysburg, there was no television or radio, internet or cell phone technology. In 1863 these were all inconceivable information sources of the future.

Likewise, there was no electricity at the time of the American Civil War. Consequentially, when citizens went to their cellars, it was dark except for sunlight through the tiny windows during the day and candlelight at night. The Gettysburg civilians were literally in the dark without much light in their cellars. But, figuratively speaking, they suffered more intense "darkness" from their lack of knowledge. Living moment to moment, they had no inkling as to how long their situation would continue, or the duration of their very lives.

Chambersburg Street proves to have been quite a diversified neighborhood. It was certainly a fortune of fate that Sarah Broadhead commenced writing a diary in June of 1863. Her account of battle week is rare since it was actually written as events were unfolding. Most recollections were put to paper many years after the actual events. That end of Chambersburg Street was also the home of one of the most famous citizens of Gettysburg, John Burns. Such a flamboyant character must have made quite an interesting neighbor. And, read on to discover who established a lemonade stand, and what problems they encountered.

John Burns sits on the porch of his home on Chambersburg Street near the west edge of town. On July 1st he "joined" the Union forces as they fought just west of town.

❖ Annie Skelly – Age 7
~33 Chambersburg Street

Since I was so young, I don't remember too much. Soldiers marched and ran down the street right in front of our house. My mother went across the street to the College Lutheran Church every day to help with the wounded. I had to stay in our neighbor's cellar most of the time since I was only seven. Our cellar was just too damp. A German man from the other end of town came to the cellar with us. He sat on a barrel and it broke because he was so heavy. We laughed when we realized what happened. We were afraid that he had been hit by a shell. It felt good to laugh.

Our battle must have been very important because President Lincoln came in November. I was standing by our Court House on Baltimore Street to watch him on his way to the cemetery. The street was filled with so many people that he could hardly pass through on his horse. He turned his head from side to side, looking very solemn. A man lifted me so that I could see him better. The President did look odd on such a small horse! Mother's main wish was to see the President. We would never forget that day!

❖ Mary McAllister- Age 40+
43-45 Chambersburg Street

Since I was over 40 and never married I was referred to as a spinster at the time of the Civil War. 1 lived on the first block of Chambersburg Street with my brother-in-law and sister, John and Martha Scott. The night of June 30th we got absolutely no sleep. Instead we watched the Rebels' campfires in the mountain to the west toward Cashtown. The next morning we were dipping water for Union soldiers as they hurried down our street. We were so excited that we burned the biscuits! Soon we were locking the doors, hoping to bar out the soldiers. However, wounded soldiers began arriving quickly. John, who had been sick, fainted at the sight of so much blood.

Martha and I made bandages and did all that we could for the wounded soldiers who were taken into College Lutheran Church across the street. I became too frightened to work when a shell hit the church — I needed to go home. Arriving home I found blood covering the front step and feared someone inside may be dead. Instead there were wounded soldiers throughout the house. Colonel Morrow of the 24th Michigan asked me to hide the sword that Confederate General Archer had surrendered to him during the battle that day. I hid this under some wood in the kitchen. He then asked me to hide his diary. That I hid inside my dress, sure that it was safe there!

Reverend Horatio S. Howell, an Army chaplain from Pennsylvania, was shot dead on the church steps right across the street. He was buried in the yard. We continued cooking and baking and caring for the wounded. We also housed five surgeons

~ 39 ~

in our home. Some Rebel soldiers came in demanding food. Martha offered them some pie, but they refused to eat it until she took the first bite. They were afraid that she was trying to poison them! This, of course, was not the case. However, we were very hungry. Mostly we had only tea and crackers. On the morning of July 4th I heard a Union band play. I think I never heard anything sweeter, and never felt so glad in my life!

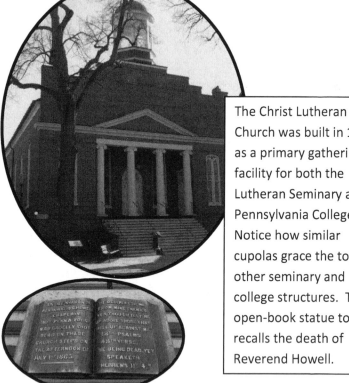

The Christ Lutheran Church was built in 1835 as a primary gathering facility for both the Lutheran Seminary and Pennsylvania College. Notice how similar cupolas grace the tops of other seminary and college structures. The open-book statue today recalls the death of Reverend Howell.

❖ Elizabeth Gilbert – Mother
213 Chambersburg Street

During the battle of Gettysburg I alone had to take care of my ten children. My husband and oldest son were both soldiers in the Union Army. We lived on the west end of Chambersburg Street in a house without a cellar. This became a problem on July 1st when officers rode through the town calling us citizens to go to our cellars for safety. During the confusion I remember an officer, although I forgot whether he was Union or Confederate, say they wanted to raise a "black flag." This meant that all those people who remained in the town would be slaughtered! Another more humane officer disagreed with the black flag because there were so many women and children like us still here. As we hurried along the street looking for safety a man opened his door and told us to come in. We stayed huddled in his cellar along with his family for three days.

During this time we saw many horrid sights. From the cellar window we could see a dead man lying on the street. When enemy soldiers passed his body they would kick him and take any clothes they needed. The water in the gutters ran tinged with blood from the many wounded. The only way we had any idea which side was winning was by the color of the pants legs running by the cellar window!

When the battle ended I was anxious to return home. Since there were still many sharpshooters in the town, a chivalrous young Rebel escorted me safely to my house. Arriving home, I found my house was a shambles. Wounded Confederate soldiers were in the front of the house while wounded Union soldiers were in the back of the house.

Even after the battle many soldiers still stayed near the town. One of my sons and a friend of his started a lemonade stand to sell drinks to the soldiers. Unfortunately, sometimes a soldier would treat his friends to lemonade then tell my son to charge it!

This 19th century view of Chambersburg Street shows the Eagle Hotel which burned to the ground in 1960 and is now replaced by a convenience store. Farther out the Chambersburg Pike at the west edge of town was the residence of Mary Thompson. Her house served as the headquarters of Confederate General Robert E. Lee of Virginia.

❖ Sarah Broadhead – Wife/Mother
217 Chambersburg Street

As a young mother living in Gettysburg during the summer of 1863 I saw many sights and sounds that I'll never forget. One night in June I got up to get a drink of water for my child when I heard a terrific noise outside. Looking out the window I saw a large fire in the distance. People were yelling that the Rebels were coming and burning as they came. Many people left our town, but I stayed. Later I was informed the fire I saw was not caused by Rebels, but any rumors were enough to frighten us then.

For the next several weeks news of the Rebels in the area kept us excited and in great suspense. On June 22nd there was a report that the enemy was in the mountains less than twenty miles away. My husband and about fifty others hurried off to cut down trees to block the mountain passages. Unfortunately the Rebels had already crossed into our valley, stealing horses and cattle as they came. Our only protection was some local militia, and I did not feel safe.

On June 26th a large force of Confederates arrived, capturing many of our soldiers. Rebel cavalry rode into town with such horrid yells that it almost frightened us to death! Believe it or not, we stood in the doorways while the enemy cavalry rode past our house! However, when the infantry soldiers walked by we closed the doors and went upstairs to look out the windows. We were afraid they might come inside and carry off everything,

What a miserable looking group they were. They wore all kinds of caps and some were barefooted. In the Diamond at the center of town the Rebel band played Southern tunes and flew their traitor's flag overhead. How humiliating this was to see.

My husband was not home to see what was happening in our town. Not imagining this would happen, he had gone to work at Hanover Junction, about 15 miles away. So, there I was alone, surrounded by thousands of enemy soldiers. I felt very uncomfortable indeed. Fortunately the Rebels marched on to York, burning our Rock Creek Bridge as they went. I heard that those dunce-like people in York actually paid the Rebel army $28,000. The Rebels couldn't cross the Susquehanna River, though, because the citizens on the other side quickly burned the bridge which ended the Rebel invasion for a time.

On the morning of June 30th my husband returned home, telling me of his capture and parole. Later Rebels came to the hill just out the Chambersburg Road and got a good look at us and we got a good look at them from our house. We thought they might shell the town at any minute. I was worried that there might be a battle soon. It was especially bad timing since I had just read in the newspaper that our Union army had a new commander. I was afraid that this would give the enemy an advantage.

I got up quite early on Wednesday, July 1[st,] to get my baking done, just in case there might be a fight. I had just put the bread into the pans when I heard cannon fire coming from the west of town. People were running here and there, screaming, not knowing what to do. My neighbors had left their home, but we decided to stay.

When the shells started to fly quite thick I took my child to the home of a friend uptown. On the way I saw Rebels who had been taken prisoner and I felt sorry for them. I was so excited by our Union artillery galloping by that for a moment I forgot to be afraid of our danger. A citizen galloped by our door and yelled for us to get into the house......we might be killed. We went to the cellar, afraid to come out even when the firing ceased. How different our town looked when we did finally emerge. Clothes, blankets, knapsacks, dead horses, and men covered our streets. The Rebels outside the house said that it would be safe to return home, so we did. I was relieved to find everything in place at our house.

Obviously I got no rest the night of July 1st. The Rebels broke into the vacated house next door and took everything they could find throughout the house, from the cellar to the garret. It was a beautiful moonlit night and we could see them load up a wagon of goods. I feared that at any minute they would come bursting through the front door of our house!

On the morning of July 2nd we again heard the roar of cannon and again we went to the cellar. Feeling hungry, my husband went to the garden to pick a mess of beans. He actually picked all the beans because he was determined that the Rebels would have none of them. Unfortunately bullets from sharpshooters were whizzing by his head as he worked. I baked some shortbread and boiled the last piece of ham in the house. Some neighbors came over and we enjoyed a nice quiet meal. I had actually been too excited and worried to eat for some time. But soon our short interlude of quiet came to an abrupt end.

At about four in the afternoon a blast came sounding like heaven and earth were being rolled together. We went to a safer cellar this time, or so we thought. A shell struck that house but luckily did not explode. The noise of battle continued until about ten o'clock at night. My husband slept soundly that night. I, on the other hand, could not eat or sleep. I continued to write in a diary that I started back in June. Then I washed out a few things for my little one. Although we could get no information about our Union Army, the Rebels were telling us that we would probably need to leave town by morning because it would be shelled. The Rebels continued to brag, although one admitted that the Union Army had the best position, the high ground south of town. The suspense kept me worried.

July 3rd brought even more loud cannonading. Again we were told to leave because the town was to be shelled. My husband refused to leave our house as long as there was one brick on top of another. We spent the afternoon in the cellar listening to the most terrible sound ever heard by human ears.

I was scared but also very sad. I realized that the sound of every shell meant death or excruciating pain for some poor soldier. If it was God's will I would have preferred to be taken away than remain to see the misery that would follow. It seemed that this awful afternoon would never come to an end. It would have eased our horror if we knew the outcome of the battle. We knew that the next day was the Fourth of July. However, we knew not what that day would bring.

On the morning of July 4th a Rebel rode down the street announcing that the Yankees were taking possession of the town. I was overjoyed to see our men in the public square. For a moment I felt safe. Then I realized that we were between the Union and Confederate lines. We felt like prisoners because we couldn't even look out the window without fear of being shot! By the end of the day the Rebels retreated and I went to bed feeling safe for the first time in a week. I was anxious to go help with the wounded the next day.

July 5th began as such a lovely day. It seemed that nature was smiling down on the thousands of suffering. It was hard to believe that man could have caused so much misery in so short a time. I went to the Seminary to help with the wounded. As I saw the horrible sights inside I thought of returning home. I entered, though, and realized I would be returning. All the wounded were hungry, and one day I realized that some soldiers were almost drowning in the cellar. They had been placed there for safety during the second and third days of battle. But the heavy rains that fell following the battle flooded the cellar floor. Their only chance for survival was to be moved to a higher level. With hard work that was accomplished. A few weeks earlier I would have fainted at the sight of blood. Now, though, I was busy working to help feed and care for the wounded.

I agreed to care for three wounded soldiers in our house. The wounded all were gentle and kind. Most churches, warehouses, and homes were being used as hospitals. The wounded Rebels were being kindly cared for as well as our own soldiers. In spite of my efforts, one of my patients died. Although he was here just a short time, I missed him. The government did not send the necessary supplies for the wounded. Fortunately the Sanitary Commission and the Christian Commission both provided well for the needy soldiers.

By July 11th our town was beginning to look more settled and familiar. However, the air was filled with the awful smell of decaying horses and human bodies not properly buried. Our house was constantly filled with strangers. One night twenty people slept in our beds and on our floors. Some were forced to stay on the street. Our little village of less than twenty- five hundred citizens was overrun and eaten out by two large armies. Then thousands of visitors came searching for loved ones in the battle. I was able to help one woman by marking the grave of her husband. He had been among the wounded I helped at the Seminary. His dying request was that I write a letter to his wife. I also sent her a lock of his hair. Her only comfort now was that she could take the body home to the resting place of his family

We citizens of Gettysburg could finally return to our ordinary lives. Our wounded were removed to hospitals. A weight of care was lifted when again we had our house to ourselves.

Sarah Broadhead fortunately commenced writing a diary in June 1863 as rumors of a Rebel invasion were rampant. She had the manuscript printed and sold some copies to help raise money for the U.S. Sanitary Commission to honor their work at Gettysburg.

❖ John Burns – Age 69
252 Chambersburg Street

I was a veteran of both the War of 1812 and the Mexican War, living peacefully as a cobbler in the town of Gettysburg at the time of the battle. When President Lincoln called for Union volunteers at the beginning of the Civil War I marched with my musket the whole way to West Chester, Pennsylvania to enlist. Imagine my disappointment when they told me I was too old to be a soldier! Although I was 68 at the time, I was as strong as a man of 50, and a great shot, to boot!

I decided to march to Hagerstown, Maryland to enlist, but was turned down again. So I joined a wagon train and became a teamster. But when I heard the sound of artillery in the distance, I took off toward the conflict. Unfortunately I arrived too late to fight in the battle of Falling Water. I continued to serve under General Banks, but winter in camp accentuated my rheumatism and other infirmities of advanced age laid me up much of the time. So, I was sent home to Gettysburg.

By spring I was ready to return to the Army, but my fellow citizens must have wanted to keep me around town. They elected me to the position of town constable. This enabled me to walk around town in my tall black fur hat and long frock coat, complete with badge. I felt that at least some of the duty of safeguarding our nation rested on my shoulders. My job remained the same until the Confederate army invaded the North and reached the vicinity of Gettysburg in late June. I immediately got my musket down and joined about 14 other townsmen who marched off to fight the enemy. Unfortunately, we were met by some Union scouts who ordered us back to town.

A few days later Confederates arrived at Gettysburg requesting supplies. As a town officer, I became so furious and violent in my language that I was held under arrest by the Confederates for two days. Sunday morning, June 28th, I was given my liberty. By that very evening I had captured and imprisoned two Confederates, including one who was carrying a message from General Ewell to General Early. On the last day of June, Union General John Buford led his Cavalry forces into town, rested them on the streets for a few hours, and then moved west toward McPherson Ridge. The two opposing armies were almost in touch with each other; a momentous battle was about to be fought right here at my town. And to think, I had marched so far to be a part of the army. Now they were coming to me!

On the morning of July 1st Buford's Cavalry was attacked and forced to fight dismounted in an attempt to hold the high ground. Just as they were being pushed back, Union General Reynolds arrived with his First Corps, but time was running out. General Reynolds asked me if there was any shortcut to quickly get his men in position to support the retreating Union Cavalry. We were able to level some fences, thus creating a direct route to Seminary Ridge through the outskirts of town. After the Union troops raced across the shortcut, I met up with some wounded soldiers, too weak to handle their guns. Hearing the roar of battle in the distance, my blood was stirred and I begged the soldiers for their guns. Soon I had not only a gun but also cartridges!

I ran across fields and fences until I came upon Stone's Union brigade hotly engaged in battle. When someone asked what I wanted, I exclaimed that I wanted a chance to shoot! Immediately I was ordered to a wooded area where the Union Iron Brigade was positioned. I soon left the timber and went to a fence in the open ground for a better-unobstructed view of the Confederates. Being a marksman, I wasted little powder while hitting the enemy. I paid most attention to mounted targets. In fact, my fellow soldiers soon were shouting suggestions as to what to shoot. They were probably a little surprised to see me there in my constable attire, shooting as calmly as at birds.

I was soon hit twice in the side, then at my belt, but I continued to shoot despite the pain. When I was hit in the leg, though, I went down. As the Confederates won the position, I found myself in a very dangerous predicament. A civilian taking part in a battle would be shown no mercy, so I tried scooping out a hole to hide my remaining ammunition. During the night I sometimes lost consciousness. As I was questioned by Confederates I replied that I was out looking for a lost girl who lived nearby when the battle started, but they didn't seem to believe my story. Around midnight it started to rain, and I became chilled. Asking for a blanket, I received one along with a drink. In the morning I must have fainted while crawling to a guard, for I awoke to find myself being cared for in a neighbor's house. That afternoon I was moved by neighbors to my own house which was also being used as a hospital.

Unfortunately, the Confederates continued to hold the town through July 2nd and 3rd. Even more unfortunately, some of my neighbors, who were Southern sympathizers, told the enemy what I just related to you. When questioned, I confessed, and immediately I was condemned to be shot! It turned out to be my good fortune that our home was totally filled with wounded soldiers. Since the two soldiers sent to do the gruesome task of doing me in couldn't find a way up to my bedroom, they decided to go to an upstairs room across the street.

From there, they shot at my bed, but I had rolled onto the floor and into an adjoining room. They didn't have time to verify if they shot me because by then they learned that Confederate General

~ 51 ~

Pickett's brave men had been torn to garments in one of the most magnificent and useless charges in the history of war. With the high hopes of the South shattered, and the invasion of the North failed, the star of the South had begun to set. So really, what did the life of this poor old bullet-riddled man signify to them?

When I finally was able to leave my bed I resumed my former responsibilities as constable of Gettysburg. Now, though, I had a new badge, a new frock coat and a white fur hat which was sent to me by someone in New York City. I am proud to say that I was now met with respect and veneration. When President Lincoln came to town he asked to see me! I requested, instead, that he come to me. Eventually I conceded and went to see the President. We walked arm in arm, from the cemetery dedication, where he spoke briefly, to the Presbyterian Church.

I still enjoyed my constable job, although I earned more as an officer of the State Senate. After my wife died I lived a very lonely life, indeed. (The preceding information was derived from a newspaper interview with John Burns. In truth, he actually lost the election for constable in March 1863. So, reader, beware of what he has to say!)

John Burns was a citizen of Gettysburg who was a civilian "soldier" on McPherson's Ridge on July 1st. His statue, shown at left, still stands there today.

&West Middle Street

How ironic! Middle Street does not run through the middle of Gettysburg. It runs east and west just one block south of the Diamond/Circle/Square. The residents of this street have quite unique stories since Middle Street became the Confederate Army's battle line for July 2nd and 3rd.

At the corner of West Middle Street and South Washington Street stands the lovely brick home of Professor Michael Jacobs and his family. As a professor of mathematics at nearby Pennsylvania College, Jacobs actually walked to the campus to teach his 8:00 morning class on Wednesday, July 1, 1863. Obviously the event that was about to unfold was not a planned affair noted on the calendar. Likewise, this dedicated professor kept thrice-daily records of the temperature. It is through his diligent efforts that we now know the temperatures during the three day battle. For example, the afternoon temperature on Friday, July 3 was 87 degrees. His actions and those of his daughter were described through a remembrance written by his son, Henry.

Such a contrast of circumstances existed, depending on one's venue. Although the Union and Confederate soldiers who were in the town of Gettysburg seemed to be courteous to the civilians, soldiers on both sides were engaged in murderous battle on fields west, north, then south of town during "Battle Week." Perhaps it was a blessing for the local citizens that "live" action news was not available on television or internet connection. Sometimes ignorance is bliss!

The remembrances of young males seem in sharp contrast to the reminiscences of females. Apparently life in Gettysburg lacked enough excitement for some boys of the area. Remember, though, these recollections were mostly written quite a long time after the actual Battle of Gettysburg. The fear factor may have diminished with time from their memories.

The Fahnestock building stands at the corner of West Middle and Baltimore Streets. In 1863 it housed the Fahnestock Brothers Dry Goods Store, one of the largest commercials enterprises in Gettysburg. As the battle began, it served as a viewing platform for Union General Howard, then later as the headquarters for the U.S. Sanitary Commission.

❖ Mary Warren – Age 12
237 West Middle Street

In late June the Confederate army marched into our town. Although many citizens of Gettysburg left their homes, we stayed. On the morning of July 1st a battle raged west of town and we heard the news that Union General Reynolds had been killed. My mother told me to go to our garret and pray. Unfortunately, the garret window offered me a view of our own Union soldiers retreating back through the town with shells bursting above them.

Later that afternoon a Confederate general took possession of our home for his headquarters. He told my father we should either leave town or go to the cellar. As we were going to the cellar, my mother asked the general if he could use the room upstairs; she had just put down a new carpet in the room where he was and she did not want it damaged. He kindly obliged her request. Although nothing in our house was disturbed, a log house just up the street was torn down for breastworks.

Confederate soldiers soon filled Middle Street in front of our house. Many lay sick and wounded in the heat, so Mother suggested they be taken to a large carriage shop nearby. She also volunteered to go and do anything she could for them. When she offered them the tea and bread she made, though, they all refused. Thinking this to be very strange, she shared with them that she had three brothers in the Union army and was treating these Confederate soldiers just as she would want her brothers to be treated. So, as she took a sip of tea, the soldiers gladly were served!

On the second day of the battle my grandfather, who lived on Baltimore Street, came to our house before sunrise to see if we needed anything. My father thought I would be safer at my grandfather's house. I will never forget that early morning walk to his house, seeing men and horses lying in the streets. While we were in my grandfather's cellar the next day we heard the awful news that young Jennie Wade was shot in a house just up Baltimore Street. And then on the next day, the Fourth of July, I saw our Union soldiers marching up that same street, hurrahing as they went. Thinking the danger to be over, and feeling rather homesick, I started toward my home. As a sharpshooter's bullet went whizzing by my ear I realized we weren't out of danger quite yet!

Arriving home, I found that the Confederates had left. However, the Union soldiers retaking the town arrested my father as a Confederate while he sat in the dining room wearing a gray suit. In order to prove his real identity he was taken up town so that other citizens could certify the truth! My mother spent much of her time baking bread, but it was all eaten by the Union soldiers by the time my father was returned safely home. A few days later my Mother wanted to bake a fruit pie, so I decided to surprise her by going out to the McMillan's farm to get some fruit. As I walked along toward the ridge west of town I passed the bodies of dead men who had probably been killed during the first day's battle. Their skin had turned a dark color as they lay dead in the scorching sunlight, and that caused me great fear.

Churches and public buildings throughout the town were used as hospitals for the many wounded soldiers. Soon an area east of town near the railroad was set up as a hospital. "Hospital Woods", as we called it for many years, was laid out along avenues with huge medical tents. During the weeks after the battle townspeople went out to see the wounded soldiers and help out when possible. In November my father took me to see President Abraham Lincoln as he dedicated ground for the final resting-place of the many Union soldiers who fell during the Battle of Gettysburg.

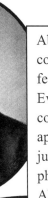

Abraham Lincoln will forever be coupled with Gettysburg. The featured dedication speaker, Edward Everett, spoke for two hours. Of course, President Lincoln's "few appropriate remarks" proved to be just that. Below is the only known photograph taken of the iconic event. Abraham Lincoln is located near the center of the picture

❖ Julia Jacobs – Age 16
103 West Middle Street

Like many other townspeople, I too spent many hours in the cellar of our house listening to the sounds of battle surround the town. Although my father and brother went outside or to the garret for better viewing of the battle, I remained inside until after the three days of battle.

On the Fourth of July, that glorious holiday, it seemed that the fighting had come to an end with the Confederates in retreat. The streets of Gettysburg were filled with a human tide of men in gray flowing like a current back to the west of town, returning toward the mountains. In an effort to cover their retreat, a group of Confederate pickets were left behind on Middle Street west of our house.

As Union soldiers rode down Washington Street and crossed Middle Street, the Confederate pickets would shoot them before they realized the danger. I watched these poor unknowing soldiers get shot right in front of our house! I could not sit back and continue to watch! I went to the threshold of the front door and stood so that Union soldiers could see me as I yelled to them of the danger. My big brother actually called me a very effective living warning system since I saved many lives.

When the Confederate pickets realized what I was doing, they started firing on me! Fortunately I got inside the hallway to safety although these marksmen hit the linden trees outside our house as they tried to silence me. I continued to cry out my warning until Union pickets built a wall to take care of the situation. Then I was treated to a rather comical duel of marksmanship as our Union pickets raised hats on swords to draw the fire of those Confederates down the street.

When we finally got to speak to some newly arrived Union soldier in front of our house, we felt our first sense of security in days. Although we saw our last episode of the battle on Sunday as General Howard and his staff rode by, the stench of the battle lingered. For weeks we had to keep our windows closed at night to avoid the awful odor of the dead men and horses. There were so many victims of our grim battle that many of their bodies lay decomposing in the fields. It was a very long time before all the victims of this grim slaughter were buried.

(In his "eyewitness account" Henry Jacobs refers to his sister as "Julia." However, her given name was Mary J., possibly after her mother "Julia.")

These images were taken by photographers who arrived after the battle. Most of the photographs of dead bodies were taken south of town since photographers arriving from Washington, D.C. arrived there first, while burial details coming from town arrived there last.

❖ Henry Jacobs – Age 18
103 West Middle Street

I was a recent graduate of Pennsylvania College, living at home with my parents during the Battle of Gettysburg. My father had taught mathematics at the college for 32 years and I was spending the summer doing preliminary reading so that I could pursue a career in the field of law. Our quiet studious town became curious and a bit apprehensive as the echoes of war came closer. None of us, though, had the slightest comprehension as to what the Confederate invasion of the North would mean to our typically unexciting little town.

On Friday, June 26th, Confederates under General Gordon took possession of our town. These men were courteous, yet firm and businesslike in their attitude towards the townspeople. Although these Confederates left our town, soon small groups of Union soldiers were coming and going through town at odd hours. We now had the growing feeling that grave events were coming our way, and we became less startled as we caught more glimpses of these actors in a drama on a stage always beyond our vision.

On Tuesday, June 30th, I decided to ease my tensions and get a clear view of the situation from our garret window. Taking a small telescope used for astronomy classes at the college, I was able to see a considerable force of Confederates west of town. Suddenly, a group of officers, who were looking in my direction, turned and rode away. Then a loud roar of shouting was heard in front of the house. Looking out the window I saw General Buford's Union cavalry arriving. Fortunately for us, their arrival stopped General Pettigrew and his men who were on their way to Gettysburg to procure shoes and other supplies. They never got the shoes that day, and many of them never needed any others afterwards.

Later that day I took the telescope to the Lutheran Theological Seminary on Seminary Hill west of town and went up into their observatory. From there I was able to see the whole horizon. Where the mountainsides of the Blue Ridge held clearings I could see smoke curling upward and soldiers attending to camp chores. As I watched the Confederate soldiers in the distant mountains, I was able to see Union soldiers below me within easy eyeshot. The tide of war was nearing. Although we were now aware of our situation, at no time during the battle did we fully realize that we were in the midst of one of the greatest battles of modern times.

On the morning of July 1st my father went to the college as usual and taught his first class from 8 to 9 o'clock. As the battle began, a Union officer from the signal corps interviewed my father. Going to the top floor of the college, which lay at the northern edge of town, my father pointed out the terrain features. He emphasized the importance of the Union army to hold Cemetery Hill. Newspapers after the battle credited him with this valuable suggestion. Soon Union General Reynolds had all the townspeople ordered to leave town. Then, with the battle beginning, the order was countermanded and we were told to stay. Although we could hear the guns booming in the distance west of town, nobody was alarmed. Around 10 o'clock I walked down to the corner of Washington Street and Chambersburg Street where I saw both General Buford and General Reynolds. As the firing seemed to be getting nearer, they rode off toward the sounds of battle. With affairs approaching a crisis, I returned home and went to the garret.

From the garret my father and I viewed the immense panorama of strife as it unrolled around our town. Union General Howard's Eleventh Corps hurried at the double-quick past our house and on toward the college. They were, indeed, a splendid vision of high courage and eager hope. However, just a few hours later we viewed a strange and awful spectacle. Those same men had been overwhelmed and beaten back in a complete rout. I saw one Union soldier, in particular, running despite his obvious exhaustion, refusing to surrender. One moment I heard one of his pursuers shouting, "Shoot him! Shoot him!" The next moment I heard the crack of a rifle shot. The Union soldier fell dead at our door. Many others died during that grim race.

Later I heard a terrible pounding on our door. It was a wounded Union soldier supported by two of his comrades who refused to leave him behind. They demanded shelter and we took them in. About half an hour later some Confederates came to the door demanding to search the house. They allowed the wounded soldier to stay, but captured his comrades who were hiding in the cellar. Later, however, they returned for the wounded soldier as well. By 5 o'clock on the afternoon of July 1st our town was fully in the enemy's possession. Although they tore down our fences to let the troops pass readily, it would be hard for anyone to criticize the conduct of the Georgians outside our house. They were courteous and considerate gentlemen who could be seen reading from their pocket Testaments.

That night was very quiet and still, despite the many wounded soldiers crowded near our home. It was as though a merciful hush had been laid on the warring passions of mankind. As I lay down to sleep in that still brooding silence I heard a solitary cry for water in a soft southern voice. He continued calling out, getting no response. I fell asleep with this anguished wailing in my ear. As I awoke the next morning I found the Confederate troops had torn down a stone wall across from our house and rebuilt it across the street to create a breastwork.

At about 4 o'clock on July 2nd our family again returned to the safety of our cellar as the sounds of artillery came from the south of town. The sounds were at times deafening, but at that point we had no idea what each phase of the firing meant. We stayed there until 8 o'clock, except for a short period of time when my father proposed that he and I go to the backyard to hear the cannonade. We made a hasty retreat back to the cellar, though, as bullets quickly started flying around us! Although we were safe, a Confederate soldier was killed as he sat on our sloping cellar door, his lifeless body gently sliding downward.

The next morning was quiet. But at exactly 1:07 by my father's watch the artillery began again, and we again returned to the safety of our cellar. We passed the afternoon listening to this cannon orchestra which seemed to be led by one especially big gun. Since we could distinguish where the firing was coming from, two ladies staying in our cellar called out, "Their side. Our side. Their side. Our side." as appropriate. When our side failed to answer, we waited anxiously.

That morning Confederate General Lee had used the college observatory to study the placement of Union forces. His shrewd eye discerned the weak point in the line to be in Hancock's Corps south of Cemetery Hill, so his artillery was focused there. When the terrific duel opened, the mind was almost dazed by the concussion. We could hear three distinctive sounds: the deep-toned growl of the gun, the shriek of flying shell, and the sharp crack of explosion. When the Union guns were silent we became very uneasy. It was as though the command had been given for the whole world to hold its breath and wait for a still greater danger.

My father returned to the garret and watched as Pickett's men swung into position. Their charge was heroic, magnificent. He called to me to come, saying, "You will see now what in your whole life you will never see again." As I looked out the garret window I saw broken remnants of Pickett's men creeping back across the cornfields. Soon a tremendous thunderstorm roared over us, but the sound seemed tame compared to what we had just heard. Later that night a great current of men again flowed down our street. By the next morning we learned that the Confederates were in retreat.

Henry Jacobs graduated from nearby Pennsylvania College in 1862 and Gettysburg Lutheran Theological Seminary in 1865. In addition to writing his remembrances of the battle, he also wrote a number of books on religion as well as the lyrics to a hymn, *Lord Jesus Christ, We Humbly Pray.*

❖ Daniel Skelly – Teenager
47 West Middle Street

June was an exciting month for the people living in and around Gettysburg. There were rumors of a Confederate invasion and people were constantly passing through our town seeking safety. Most of our merchants had shipped their goods to Philadelphia. The store where I worked, Fahnestock Brothers, kept a train car available at all times to send our goods to safety. We would simply go out of business until things settled down along the border. Then the merchandise was brought back and we continued with our usual routine. The Confederates did appropriate a shipment of gloves while the train passed through Hanover Junction. An unfortunate jeweler waited too long getting out of town and thus had his stock appropriated.

By the end of June we knew for sure that Confederate troops were in the area. From our rooftops we could see their campfires in the mountains. Oddly enough, we felt quite safe when General Buford finally arrived with Union cavalry on June 30th. I watched him as he sat astride his horse on Chambersburg Street. He seemed very calm and soldierly, although his uniform was different than any I had ever seen. It was like a hunting coat of blouse effect. The citizens of Gettysburg enjoyed a sense of security that night, not imagining what was in store for them in the very near future.

Early on the morning of July 1st I walked with a friend out toward Seminary Ridge. The ridge was full of men and boys from the town. I guess we were all eager to witness a brush with the enemy. I could not have dreamed that such a large conflict was about to begin. I climbed a sturdy oak tree to get a better view.

From there I was able to witness Buford's men fight dismounted like infantry against the Rebels. Soon shots began to fly over our heads and there was a stampede toward the town. A cannonball struck the earth less than twenty feet from me, scattering the ground. This caused me to quicken my pace considerably!

The streets of town were filled with men, women, and children, all bursting with excitement. I went to the roof of the Fahnestock building and got a good view of the continuing battle west of the town. Noticing a Union General riding down Baltimore Street, I invited him up to observe the situation. General Howard used his field glass to survey the land and also notice the number of roads that radiated from the town like spokes on a wheel. A scout arrived with information that General Reynolds had been killed. General Howard calmly gave many orders, but one that I remember most concerned music. He wanted bands to be placed at the head of the columns and play lively airs as they advanced.

Later I went to the center of town and saw my mother carrying two buckets of water to the wounded. This seemed quite ironic since two of my brothers had recently been captured by the Confederates at the Battle of Winchester. Later we found out that one was mortally wounded and died. During the battle of Gettysburg, though, my mother and most of the other townspeople worked hard to bring relief to the suffering soldiers. My neighbor, Julia Culp, helped with the wounded at the nearby courthouse. She also had two soldier brothers, one who fought for the Union army and one who fought for the Confederate army. Some of the men that I helped were so frightfully wounded that a lady could not go near them. By late afternoon our forces were being driven back through the town. I went home feeling that everything was lost. I never in my life felt so depressed.

That night the Confederates formed a line of battle in front of our house. We were in the hands of the enemy! The Confederate soldiers displayed perfect discipline and always asked my mother for permission to use our kitchen stove. That night passed very quietly. The enemy slept just outside below our windows, and we enjoyed a good night's rest as well.

We had no idea what to expect on July 2nd. We cautiously went out on the street. I started a conversation with a Confederate soldier who showed my General Lee as he rode by. The soldier and I talked about the causes of the war and the effects on both sides. Our conversation was interrupted by cannonading south of town. Since our town was cut off from the outside world we were in the dark as to what was actually happening to our army. This time we went to a larger cellar for safety. When we later came upstairs we were quite shocked. A neighbor had left a bandbox containing a bonnet setting on a chair where she had been sitting. A Minnie ball had passed through the box and the bonnet!

On the night of the second I slept in a room above the Fahnestock store with some other boys. I remember how we sat quietly by the windows, trying desperately to hear what the Confederates were saying on the street below. We were eager to catch a clue as to how our Union army was doing. We finally did fall soundly asleep as boys do who have few cares and good health. Several times during the night we were awakened by musketry firing.

Heavy firing awoke us on July 3rd, but the rest of the morning was quiet. About 1:30 in the afternoon, though, pandemonium broke loose. For several hours there was the tremendous sound of a cannonade followed by an ominous calm. I went out on the street trying to find out what this all meant, but could get no information. The artillery then opened fire for some time. I was very restless and unable to sleep as I went to bed that night. Early in the morning I went to the window to see the cause of the loud noise. It was our boys in blue marching down the street to the musical accompaniment of a fife and drum corps with our Stars and Stripes flag waving. Later that day I ventured out to mingle with our neighbors and compare notes about how they fared at the hands of our friends, the enemy.

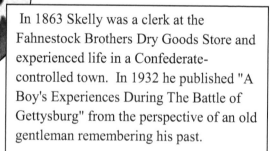

In 1863 Skelly was a clerk at the Fahnestock Brothers Dry Goods Store and experienced life in a Confederate-controlled town. In 1932 he published "A Boy's Experiences During The Battle of Gettysburg" from the perspective of an old gentleman remembering his past.

❧York Street, Carlisle Street and Pennsylvania College

Although the eastern and northern sections of Gettysburg were less involved in the Battle of Gettysburg, citizens living there were still impacted. The topic of food, and lack of food, has been mentioned by several previous citizens. In this section Mrs. Sarah King will express the need for food to feed her hungry family. Likewise, college student T.F Shuey expresses an intense hunger.

Mrs. King and Emma Yount's accounts mention several places of interest within and around the town. Emma lived right across the street from the recently- built train station. Certainly she never expected such an important traveler as the President of the United States to arrive in Gettysburg. She also mentions the Washington House, an inn for travelers. Being a crossroads town, Gettysburg boasted The Globe, the Eagle Hotel, and others.

Mrs. King mentions the Poor House, just north of town. There was no Social Security or nursing homes in 1863, so as citizens of Adams County would become needy or aged, they could be moved to this facility. Although the buildings were torn down during the 1960's, the graveyard for the Alms House is still located on Barlow's Knoll.

The account written by college student Shuey is especially unique. He mentions being a new student, thus he actually didn't know the name of the president of Pennsylvania College. In his original reminiscences he referred to President Baker, instead of the actual President Baugher. Shuey does a remarkable job of expressing the impact on and the importance of the college family and facility during the battle.

❖ Sarah King – Wife and Mother of Five
165 York Street

General Ewell's division of Confederate soldiers passed by our house on Friday, June 26th. I must admit, that as I watched from my porch, I felt sympathy for those men. They seemed ragged, and had a look of hunger in their eyes. Their appearance told plainly of their indescribable suffering and deprivation. Some of them spoke to the children as they marched by. In fact, one of them asked my son if he would like to shoot a Rebel!

Two Confederate soldiers came to our door asking for food. They came one at a time though, not in company. They each wanted me to sell them bread, but I would not do so. Instead, I gave one a loaf of bread along with some butter, instructing him to share with the other. As they sat eating on the porch across the street, my neighbor heard them express their surprise that our citizens were so kind to them, considering they came to kill our husbands and sons. Ewell's Confederate division marched on to York, a larger town thirty miles to the east, hoping more supplies would be available there.

Each day we returned to our porch, watching and listening for news of more Rebels. On July 1st I heard a Union Cavalry soldier say, "Well, the ball is about to open." From this comment I concluded that a battle was to take place close by, so I prepared some things to carry with us if we had to leave town. My father had brought me some blueberries that morning, so I went to the basement and made some pies. He had bought them from Billy Noel, a countryman, who had come to town ignorant to the fact that a battle loomed in the near future. Upon hearing the news, he kindly offered us shelter at his cabin on Wolf Hill south of town.

As I filled a peck basket of biscuits, Mother visited up town. Upon returning she reported that all was excitement there. I then went down to the Gilbert house where wounded soldiers had been taken. As I did what I could to relieve the suffering, we received word that our own General Reynolds had been killed. Meanwhile, my little folks went next door to pick lint for bandages. Soon the fighting got so close to our house that a soldier on horseback ordered us to our cellars for safety.

My father proposed that he stay at the house and that Mother and I and my five children go to the toll gate house about half a mile away. Dressing my children in their most substantial clothing, I put on my best garb. I was finally realizing that our situation was more serious than I had believed. I filled the pocket as well as the bosom area of my dress with articles too numerous to mention. I filled a basket with cakes and bread and shawls, in case we would have to be out of doors over night. By this time I heard there was fighting just north of town in Poor House Woods. Although I tried to see this battle, there was too much smoke.

The next day at the toll gate house we heard shells falling all around us. Someone had to go tend to the young stock, some colts and young cattle, up in the barn. One of the ladies was upstairs baking when some Rebels came to the door and told her we would all be killed if we stayed. She came to the cellar door to inform us of this news. Since she decided that she was going to stay (reasoning that she would probably be killed if she left, so she would rather die at home), we also stayed where we were.

Returning home on July 4th, my room seemed undisturbed except for a small pile of gray rags. Later I realized that my husband's fine blue suit, which he had received as a Christmas present, was missing from a storage trunk. Apparently, the gray rags were left in exchange! I gathered them up with a stick and threw them out in the street. I soon learned of a young wounded Rebel who needed clothing, and he was requesting gray. His caregiver, Miss Jane Moore who was an independent nurse from Baltimore, wanted to gratify his wish. So, I took the ragged hat, pants, and shirt to her. They were just the thing he requested and greatly appreciated.

This drawing by Alfred Waud depicts the death of Gen. Reynolds at Gettysburg, July 1, 1863. Waud served as an illustrator for Harper's Weekly and was one of only two artists known to be present at the battle of Gettysburg. The local residents had no technology to get up-to-the-minute images of the turbulent battles raging around them.

❖ Emma Yount – Age 7
32 Carlisle Street

I got to throw a bouquet to President Lincoln! I was only seven years old when he came to our town. He arrived by train at the train station across the street from my family's hotel, the Washington House. He came to town in November to dedicate a cemetery for the burial of our soldiers killed in the great battle last summer. Just before the battle our street filled with soldiers, but I wasn't afraid of them. I played out on the pavement like I always do. A soldier sitting on our doorstep asked me to come and talk to him. He said that he had a little girl at home and was afraid he might never see her again. He knew there would be a battle soon so he asked if I would kiss him for her. I asked my mother and she said, "Yes, under the circumstances." I kissed him and he gave me a beautiful silk handkerchief! It had a red, white and blue border around a picture of George Washington! I shall keep it forever. And, I will always wonder what happened to the soldier who gave it to me. I wonder if he ever saw his own little girl again.

Oh, I almost forgot to tell you about the President. He stayed at the home of Lawyer Wills, just about a block from my house. He traveled to and from Gettysburg by train. As he was leaving, I stood right under his open train window. Since I am so short another girl had to help me throw my bouquet high enough. I can't even remember if he spoke or just bowed to me. It was so noisy I couldn't have heard him anyway. I still wonder if he dedicated the grave of the soldier I kissed. I guess I shall never know.

❖ Nellie Auchinbaugh- Daughter
104 Carlisle Street

The summer of 1863 in Gettysburg was one of work and misery. For parts of three days our small town here in the Union state of Pennsylvania was held by the enemy. The Confederate soldiers ordered us townspeople to make coffee and gingerbread to send to the hospitals. That was actually the easiest task. We also needed to assist with helping the many wounded who were crowded into our homes and churches.

Some of my worst memories include my uncle's store. There I saw soldiers who were so hungry that they stole mackerel fish. These fish were kept in barrels of salt water and the solders ate them— heads, tails, and all. Later the store was turned into a hospital. Many soldiers were so badly wounded that their arms or legs were amputated. There were so many limbs that the pile reached up to the window sill.

While I was a nurse I actually helped a surgeon with a lung surgery. Unfortunately I started to feel faint and had to leave. On my way out of the hospital I gave my basin to a new friend I had met. She had come to Gettysburg after the battle looking for her sweetheart. Finally she gave up her search and decided to help take care of the wounded. As fate would have it, she took my place in the surgery and the patient was her sweetheart! He lived just a few days but did recognize her presence by his side.

❖ Charles Schick – Age 7
125 Carlisle Street
(Father's Store was located at 1 Baltimore Street)

I was only seven years old when one of the great battles of history was fought in my town. The concussion of the cannonade, the whining of countless rifle bullets, the groans of dying men, and the pitiful whinnies of wounded horses often have recurred in my ears since those terrible days. I can still hear the clattering of cavalry hoofs and the ringing of sabers from the cavalry fight I witnessed by Rock Creek east of town. After the three days of battle came a heavenly barrage in the form of a big rain storm. How amazing that storm made such a great impression on me as a child in the midst of warfare.

Up until 1861, life in Gettysburg was very humdrum for my family. My father had been born in the town and was a dry goods merchant. When the Civil War began groups of good friends and families were split wide open on the issues of the conflict. Men folk went away to serve and even kill each other in the opposing armies. Citizens of Gettysburg had no reason to believe the conflict would actually touch their peaceful community. Then in late June of 1863 there were signal fires sighted on the ridges west and northwest of the town. I remember being more impressed, though, by the arrival of soldiers! When I saw a federal cavalry officer killed, then trampled by his horse on one of our main streets, I ran home in terror. Curiosity soon overcame my childish fears and I remember going up on our balcony with my twelve-year-old sister Mary. We watched as our Union forces were overcome and forced to retreat. As Union

General Howard arrived he looked up at Mary who was waving a small American flag. He saluted the flag and urged his men onward. That tiny flag seemed to restore the morale of the others, too.

By July 2nd I was down cellar with the rest of my family. That morning a cannonball came through the roof of our house and plunged through to the second floor. My father poured bucket after bucket of water on that red-hot missile in order to cool it off. The third day, still in enemy hands, my father learned some frightening news from some friendly "Johnny Rebs" who he had been feeding out of our cellar. Our house had been ordered blown up because Confederates suspected that Union sharpshooters were being harbored here. We fled to the home of my grandfather, but he lived only a short distance from Cemetery ridge where Pickett made his famous charge. As I heard those two cannon blasts which signaled the start of the cannonade, I saw my father stand silently with arms folded and head bowed

As a result of the Battle of Gettysburg I became quite a talented drummer. I beat the muffled sad roll for innumerable funeral processions on a toy drum my father gave to me.

(This account is based on a Chicago newspaper article from July of 1938 during the 75th battle anniversary. He was employed by the New York Life Insurance Company and living in Chicago, Illinois at the time of the interview. The Schick house in Gettysburg has been replaced with another structure.)

❖ T.F. Shuey – Student
Pennsylvania College

I was a college student at the time of the Battle of Gettysburg and kept a diary of the events using my skills of shorthand and a pencil. Arriving in Pennsylvania only a few days before Lee's invasion, I hurried to the state capital at Harrisburg to enlist in the only service that seemed open to me, the state militia. I was assigned to a regiment encamped near Gettysburg, but before I arrived that unit was dispersed and partially captured by the Rebels. While waiting with some other college students to learn the whereabouts of our regiment, the battle opened.

On Wednesday morning, as we heard the Rebels commence cannonading, a party of six of us left the town for the purpose of seeing the fight. We returned to the cemetery where we had a considerable shower of rain. Then it became too hot for us in the cemetery….that is, the shells commenced falling pretty close to us. We made a flank movement and stopped by a house to procure something to eat. After this we found a better position with an excellent view of the battle. As it became too warm for us, we shifted our position. When we found out that the body of Union General Reynolds was being guarded in a house near the cemetery, we went to have a look. We were not permitted to view it as we desired, though.

During the day many shells passed very near to us. At about 4:30 our army commenced falling back and we made another flank movement, this time passing though the retreating army! As the Federals fell back, the Rebels took possession of the town. My friends and I ended up in a woods along with some Union stragglers who told us there were enemy soldiers at the other edge of the woods. Fearing this area would be shelled, we hurried along. About a mile away we came to a house where we took supper. As we entered the town we again came in contact with Rebels. They seemed very social, but thought only of taking possession of the cemetery the next morning. We slept in the college as usual that night, but wounded soldiers occupied the lower floor. The entire building was heavily guarded and none but students were permitted to enter.

The next morning was very foggy. We could hear the armies occasionally interchange salutations by means of bombshells with an occasional fire of musketry. By noon, though, there was skirmishing all along the lines. The college was taken as a hospital and a red flag was raised overhead. Little attention was being paid to the Federal wounded here and many were dying. It is hard to believe that at 2:00 in the afternoon I wrote an entry in my diary stating, "From the present aspect of affairs, I think it doubtful whether there will be a fight today." I was actually thinking about my hunger. The enemy had destroyed our boarding house yesterday and eatables were very scarce in town. At 4:30 the cannon opened with a terrible fire. I continued writing in my diary amid the thundering volleys of cannon.

By 6:30 the Rebels had silenced the better part of our batteries and our army was forced to retreat. The weather was calm and clear as the battled raged more fiercely than ever at 7:00. The Federals seemed reanimated as they fought in desperation, contesting every inch of ground. By 8:30 there were only two of us students remaining at the college, and we went to President Baker's (Baugher's) cellar for protection after a shell exploded on the campus. Later that night we returned to our college building to attend to some Federal wounded, then again went to President Baugher's house. This time we slept in a room with open windows facing the armies. We slept soundly until awakened by thundering cannon and musketry sounding in every direction.

The firing on Friday morning commenced about daylight. We arose about five and immediately visited our old position on the third floor of the college. The Rebels were saying they had not known such obstinate resistance on the part of our Union forces since the war started. A good many Federal prisoners were taken, but our forces still held the cemetery which was impregnable.

The cannonading stopped about 10:00 that morning. I, in the company of about a dozen other college students, was very busy removing books from the college library and the carpets from the literary halls. Around 1:00 cannonading commenced very briskly and by 3:30 the Rebels had undoubtedly retreated a considerable distance. Those Rebels around the college seemed very much excited. We learned that their army made a desperate attempt to take the cemetery, but it was defeated. The fighting did not seem as heavy today, although there was cannonading. It seemed the Rebels were evidently worsted.

The next day, Saturday, July 4, I awoke after a refreshing sleep to find the Federal troops back in town. With this battle finished, I soon afterwards entered the volunteer service and served to the close of the war as a private in the Union Army of the James. Unfortunately, history never seemed to credit the Army of the James with all of the hard fighting that it actually did.

❧Seminary Ridge and West of Town

Gettysburg was, and is, probably the only town that is situated amid a Cemetery Ridge and a Seminary Ridge. The Evergreen Cemetery was established in 1854 on a hill at the southern edge of town, thus creating Cemetery Hill. The ridge extending farther southward took the name of Cemetery Ridge. Both of these high positions were utilized by the Army during the Battle of Gettysburg.

In 1826 Reverend Samuel Schmucker established a Lutheran Theological Seminary in Gettysburg. In1832 Seminary structures were built on a ridge west of town, thus providing the name Seminary Ridge. During the years of the American Civil War Reverend Schmucker was a staunch abolitionist, well-known through his writings. This ridge was home to his educational institution, his lovely brick house, and to a "station" on the Underground Railroad." Slaves were able to escape to safety in the North by traveling under darkness of night from station to station. How ironic this ridge became the Confederate position during the Battle of Gettysburg.

The reminiscences of the following citizens contain a wealth of battle information as well as an abundance of emotional excitement. The word "drama" and other vocabulary referring to stage productions are apparent in several accounts. Many seemed to write as members of the audience. Likewise, the phrase "Our friends the enemy" was repeated by several of our citizen authors. Apparently being surrounded by the Confederates and relying on them for information as well as your safety made them "friends" during this trying time. Certainly in many cases the citizens and the enemy soldiers established a symbiotic relationship out of the necessity of circumstances.

Although few houses in town were purposely destroyed by the Confederates, at least one home was burned just west of town. And, although most citizens either left the area or remained in their cellars, some folks dared to be different, risking their lives for others.

How rare that a mother and son each wrote a recollection. Their opposing points of view again remind us how some things never change. What boy wants to wear a coat, and what mother doesn't issue that reminder? The reference Billy Bayly makes to "John Gilpin speed" refers to a literary figure whose image is now on the Caldecott Medal which is awarded each year for the best illustrated children's book.

This photograph is a view of Gettysburg as viewed from Seminary Ridge west of town. The road is the Chambersburg Pike heading east toward the Diamond.

❖ Lydia Ziegler - Age 13
Lutheran Theological Seminary

Pandemonium broke out in our quiet little town. Early in June the citizens of Gettysburg became very disturbed with rumors that the enemy had crossed the Potomac River. Farmers took their livestock to a safer place and merchants either hid their valuable goods or shipped them to safety. Anxiety filled every breast.

Since my father was the steward at the Lutheran Seminary, we lived on the first floor of the dormitory building. I shall never forget seeing a Confederate host marching in the Chambersburg Pike as I stood with my parents on the steps of Schmucker Hall. Such ragged men I never saw before in my life. They searched the Seminary building looking for Union soldiers.

Later, Union soldiers did arrive, and what a royal welcome we gave them! I was so happy to hand out the cakes and pies that Mother had baked. The soldiers were quite hungry for some home victuals. That night I remember going up into the cupola and getting a panoramic view of the area. Campfires of the enemy were burning in the distance along the South Mountains. Our boys were busy writing letters, praying, and singing hearty patriotic songs. Many of them seemed oblivious to the threatening dangers.

The morning of July 1st began as a beautiful day. We arose early to help feed the soldiers. Along about eight o'clock, though, shots were heard toward the mountains. We knew this meant the beginning of a battle and we were terrified! Our soldiers fell into line and marched across the fields to the sounds of music. I had always wanted to see a battle, so I slipped into the woods behind the Seminary to get a better look. A bullet flew so near my head that I could hear it whizzing! I hurried back home and found my family had gone to the cellar for safety. It was a good thing, too, because two shells hit the house.

Soon our Union Army started to fall back through the town! My father said that we should go with them so as not to fall into enemy hands. We quickly gathered up some food and left. Our march into town was heart-sickening. Wounded soldiers lay groaning and suffering at our feet. We saw first-hand what a terrible thing war can be.

The town wasn't safe so we went to Culp's hill, but that wasn't safe either. We went to Spangler's spring, but shells and bullets drove us out of there, too. Heavy rains drenched us to the skin and we were so tired. Mother had brought along bread that she divided among us, and we picked wild raspberries. I think this was the best meal I ever had. Our faithful old dog, Sport, was with us. We had to carry him as we hurried on to yet a safer place. He licked our hands to show his gratitude.

We finally found safety at the home of a friend who lived near the village of Two Taverns. We stayed there until the fighting had ended. Our friend gave us bread to eat when we returned home. That bread certainly didn't last until we got home, though. The whole way home there were wounded and hungry soldiers who had not eaten in days. The dead and the dying were all around us, both men and beasts. We saw twenty dead horses lying in a row. This pen cannot describe the awful sights and smells of that day. All day we tried to do what we could to help those who were suffering.

~ 83 ~

When we finally got home we found that all of our things had been taken. There were no beds and no clothes! Luckily, our two beautiful white cows were still alive. But, all of our hogs were killed. Our home had been turned into a hospital, so we went to work caring for the wounded and dying soldiers. Many times I received the last messages of dying fathers and husbands for their loved ones at home. Even when I did small acts of kindness for these men they would respond, "God bless you, my girl."

One day an elderly couple approached our house, the hospital. They said that four of their sons had been killed in the war. They came looking for their only other son who had been in the battle of Gettysburg. They had walked over twenty miles over the mountain from Chambersburg with things they knew their son liked. The name of their son was Charlie and he was indeed in our house. Charlie was able to see his parents just before he died and they were able to take his body home.

Our home and town would never be the same. Many of our belongings were destroyed but we received nothing from the government.

❖ Harriet Bayly – Wife and Mother
Newville Road (now Table Rock Road)

What a summer! I knew there was going to be trouble ahead as soon as we heard that Lee's Army had crossed the Potomac River. We expected the raiding and the foraging, but we certainly didn't expect the battle. My husband and thirteen- year-old son set out to take our horses to a safer place. I stayed at home and even went to Sunday school, but the elders and children were both too excited to stay. The Rebels arrived much too quickly. Although my husband hurried home to see if everything was all right, some hungry Confederates had already stopped for food.

The day before the battle was like the time before a storm... everybody was anxious about what might happen. That night we could see the campfires of the enemy along the Blue Ridge Mountains. The next morning we hurried through the chores and went our separate ways. My uncle stopped by and wanted me to go with him to see what was happening. We hadn't gone far when we heard the first cannon shots. As if by magic, thousands of soldiers rose from the earth! We ran toward home, terrorized, but my uncle was captured by Rebel cavalry. Then, I too was captured. I was asked if I knew where the Yankees were located and how many there were. I told them that I did not stop to count them. They told me that I was in a very dangerous position, and I certainly had to agree. They soon allowed me to continue home, though.
Everything at home was in a state of confusion. Rebels were constantly demanding food. They wanted to take our unbroken colts in the meadow. But luckily for us, they couldn't catch them! They did kill our chickens, most of our steers, and about one hundred sheep. I spent most of my time cooking for

these unwanted guests who swarmed all over the place. My sons were there to help, but my husband had not returned home. I was afraid that he had been taken prisoner.

That night we closed up the house and went to bed. In the middle of the night there was a knock at the door. We opened it to find a young Rebel soldier, still a teenager. He said that he never intended to do any more fighting for the Confederates. We gave him civilian clothes and he hid in our house. He said he planned to stay in the area and never return to the South. Actually, quite a few Rebel soldiers straggled behind and never went south with Lee's Army.

During the second day of the battle I took supplies to those wounded on the battlefield of the first day. They lay in the scorching sun with no food and no water. I asked a Confederate officer how he could stand to hear the pitiful cries and not help. He replied that the well at the nearest house had been pumped dry. I directed them to a nearby spring and soon there was plenty of water. In addition to helping the wounded I assisted the prisoners. They swarmed around me like bees, begging me to take charge of their letters to family and friends. When I finally did get home that day I found my husband had returned unharmed and that he had been worrying about me!

Of course the battle raged on for yet another day. The defeated Rebels returned to our farm again for our horses. This time they even took Nellie, which broke my heart. She had been the pet of my little daughter who recently passed away. The soldier who took her said that he really despised the whole business and would leave her if he could. I knew we would never see Nellie again. The roar of the cannon, the shriek of the shell, and the rumble of wagons has stopped. Finally we can live in peace again.

❖ Billy Bayly – Harriet's 13- year-old Son Newville Road (now Table Rock Road)

My summer was one of great excitement and wonder! For three days thousands of soldiers battled right near our house. I do believe the adults around here were worried because they understood the danger and possible consequences. I felt like I was seeing a great dramatic play. I had the opportunity to learn a lot about the thoughts and feelings of our friends the enemy.

The war actually started to affect our life here on the farm last summer. We could faintly hear the guns at the battle of Antietam down in Maryland. And, there were always rumors that the enemy was approaching Pennsylvania. Once my family was so alarmed that we took some of our horses and skedaddled up to Harrisburg. There we felt safe as we stayed in a large barn. While we were there we helped the farmer harvest his wheat crop. After a few days we felt it was safe to return home. What a welcome surprise it was to find that a group of skedaddlers from Maryland had stayed in our barn and had harvested and stacked our wheat crop!

In late June we were out in the field haying when a rain came and we had to go back to the house. Upon returning home we were informed of a rumor that Rebels were approaching. I guess I wasn't too worried because I found a comfortable spot in the house and took a nap. But soon my father woke me to help him take the animals to safety. My mother ran from the house with shoes and a coat for me, but I didn't take time to put them on. I rode off on our one horse named Nellie at John Gilpin speed. That night we stayed in a barn and I slept quite well. In the morning, however, Confederate cavalrymen appeared and I felt like we were rats in a trap. While some of the men argued, we got ourselves and our horses to safety and continued on our way. It soon seemed the Rebels were everywhere, so we returned home.

On the morning of July 1st nothing seemed to indicate what was about to happen. My father went on an errand to town and my mother went to help a sick neighbor. I decided to head off to town with some of my friends. There we stood in Gettysburg in our bare feet as we watched the Union army arrive. How glorious and exciting that was! We started home, just because it seemed the right thing to do. Then we decided to stop and pick raspberries. We forgot all about the rumors of war until we heard the blast of cannon. Noticing that the cannon balls were coming in our direction we continued homeward. But we found that the top rail of a fence provided perfect seating to view the battle. We sat and drank in the melody of the battle.

There came a point that conditions got a little too hot even for our comfort and we considered going home. We thought perhaps our mothers may be worried, and mothers are entitled to our consideration. So, we went home. Neither of my parents was there. So, since I was the oldest responsible male member of the family, I took charge. I must admit it was hard to take care of the necessary responsibilities when I wanted to be watching the battle!

Mother finally did get home safely. Immediately she was put to work making chicken soup, baking bread, and preparing cherry pies for hungry Rebel soldiers who came by. We were very worried about father, hoping that he had not been taken a prisoner. That night there was a knock at the kitchen door and mother told me to follow her downstairs. At the door was a Rebel who was just about my size but a bit older. He said that his North Carolina unit had been cut to pieces and that he was tired of fighting. Since he never wanted to see another battle again he asked if my mother would hide him until the battle was over. We gave him clothes to replace his uniform and hid him in the garret where the feather beds were stored for the summer.

On the second day of battle I picked cherries while my mother went out to the field of the first day's battle to care for the wounded. I was especially glad to see my father arrive home safely. The responsibility as head of the house had begun to wear on me! My father was especially glad to see my mother arrive home safely. None of us were glad to see Rebels soldiers at our door again, asking for food and telling us how badly they had whipped our Yankee soldiers. We could only hope that our Union Army could take advantage of the high ground that they now held south of town.

During the afternoon a neighbor woman dropped by for my mother's recipe for chopped pickle. I went to the sitting room for the recipe book and left the desk open. A Rebel soldier in the room apparently saw a $20 greenback note in the desk because it was soon gone. Of course, this was only one of many belongings that we would never see again.

The most impressive incidents of the battle came that evening. There was a constant thunder of artillery and flashes of fire from bursting shells. I had the opportunity to crawl out on my porch roof and take in these sights and sounds that I shall never forget. During that day I had been too busy responding to the countless demands on my services. I was beginning to feel that I was not getting my money's worth of the show. The roar of the cannons was enough to make the windows rattle and the house shake. It is a pity that I cannot put into words just what I felt that night. I do remember that the silence that finally came was almost as incredible as the noise.

Later that night several Confederate officers asked to spend the night in our house. They were given the spare room. Although they kept their door closed that night, they left their swords and pistols in the hallway. The thought crossed my mind to grab the weapons and run, or maybe capture the Confederates. I guess my common sense took over when I realized what could possibly happen to my family if my plan failed.

The third day was pretty much like the first two. Our guests insisted that the Yanks were still being whipped, but we could see a great change in their tempers. Soon there was a drift of wagon trains westward, back from which they came, even while a battle was raging just south of town. Two of my cousins participated during the fighting the previous day and one lay wounded in a field hospital back of Big Round Top. Of course, we didn't know that at the time. In fact, we didn't realize that the next day, the glorious Fourth of July, would be relatively quiet.

❖ Amelia Harman – Student
Mill Road (now Old Mill Road)

I was a still a school girl attending Miss Sheads' female academy, the Oakridge Seminary, located on the Chambersburg Pike. At that time I was living with my aunt at the "Old McLean Place" which was owned by Reverend Charles McLean. It was located on the highest point of the bluff just west of Willoughby Run.

My aunt and I were probably the only two people on the Union side who were fed by General Lee's Confederate commissary during the Battle of Gettysburg. We were also probably the only two people to have their house set on fire deliberately by the enemy. Although most of our neighbors had abandoned their homes, we decided to stay because our house was a colonial mansion of the old-fashioned fortress type with 18- inch walls and heavy wooden shutters. Since the man who farmed for us had taken the horses to the hills in the hope of hiding them, we were home alone when the fighting began.

The ominous booming of cannon began at about nine o'clock the morning of July 1st. Rushing to the windows we beheld hundreds of galloping horses coming up the road, through the fields, and even past our very door. Boom! The cannons spoke again, and more horses and their riders hurried by, yelling and shouting to each other. The road was alive with the enemy! We later found out that we were in the very center of the first shock of the battle. Filled with terror, we locked all the doors, rushed upstairs, and threw open the shutters of the west window. With our first glance, a minnie ball crashed into the shutter very close to my aunt's ear. Truly, only a thickness of paper stood between her and death.

It took just one glance at our large timothy field, between the barn and the woods, to see it partially concealed hundreds of gray crouching figures as they stealthily advanced. We shrieked out to a Union cavalry soldier, "Look. The field is full of Rebels." Someone immediately yelled up to us, "Leave the window or you will be killed." Without needing a second warning, we rushed up to the cupola. From there we could see the landscape around us unrolled like a panorama. It was as though the fields and woods had been planted with dragons' teeth. Where flowers and grass grew only an hour ago, now there were armed soldiers.

Although we didn't know it at the time, we saw the quick, sharp engagement nearby where Union General Reynolds fell. This had hardly ended when we saw a dark sinuous line of soldiers winding beyond the town, like a giant serpent. It was the Union Army advancing on the double quick! Suddenly, a violent commotion below made us fly in quick haste to the lower floor. We heard tumultuous pounding on the kitchen door and yells of, "Open or we will break down your doors." As we drew open the bolt, in poured a stream of maddened and powder-blackened soldiers in blue uniforms. They ordered us to the cellar while they went to the windows. From our cellar prison we could hear the constant crack of rifles and hurried orders. Outside the roar of muskets mingled with yelling troops and occasional cannon booms.

The suspense and agony of uncertainty were awful. Above all this confusion, though, we could hear the beating of our own hearts. I don't remember exactly how long this lasted. But then, all of a sudden, there came a scurrying of quick feet, a clattering on the stairs, the slamming of doors, and then for an instant there was silence. With a sickening dread, we waited for the next act in the drama. Soon there was a swish on the front lawn, like the mowing of grass. Then a dense shadow darkened the cellar window. It was the shadow created by hundreds of marching feet! Although we could only see them up to the knee, their gray uniforms told us they were Confederates. Now we realized that our Union soldiers, forced to retreat, had left the house, leaving us alone to face our fate!

We rushed up the steps to find our house filled with Rebels. Already our barn was ablaze and now soldiers were deliberately torching our house. They used our own newspapers for kindling, and then piled on books, rugs, and furniture. My aunt and I jumped on the fire, hoping to extinguish it. Although we pleaded with those Rebels to spare our home, there was no pity in their determined faces. They boasted that they were the Louisiana Tigers, and that we would burn with the house if we did not get out. (It seems historically unlikely that Louisiana troops were in this area.) Fleeing our house we endured even worse horrors as we found ourselves between the Union and Confederate battle lines!

Going to town would have been like walking into the jaws of death. Our only open path was westward through the ranks of the Confederate Army to safety in the rear. As we ran bullets whistled past our ears, and shells burst scattering their deadly contents. All around us wounded men were falling. My aunt and I were objects of wonder and amazement! Few took time to listen to our story, and nobody believed it. When we had gone about two miles we came to a group of officers and newspaper men. As we told our story the newspaper men listened attentively, but the others were incredulous.

I think the only one who credited our story fully was the Confederate correspondent from the London Times. He courteously walked with us to safety and assured us that the ruffians who fired our house would meet with punishment at the hands of General Lee. He placed us in an empty cottage which was quite close to General Lee's headquarters. We were promised reimbursement for our losses, in Confederate money, of course. General Lee placed a guard outside and sent us rations every day that the terrible battle continued. Each day we were furnished with bread, bacon and coffee. Although the guard was most respectful, those days were full of suspense and dread. Our nights were filled with horror. What would morning bring?

On the morning of July 4th there was no breakfast. Our guard had vanished. We didn't eat until late that afternoon when we finally came to an inhabited house. There we were cordially welcomed by the editor of the "Gettysburg Compiler" newspaper who urged us to stay overnight. The next afternoon we footed it "home" since there was not a horse or vehicle to be found in the entire county. I will not even describe the sickening sights we passed. I wish that I myself could forget them. Reaching the site of our home, a prosperous farmhouse five days earlier, there appeared only a blackened ruin and the silence of death. Here I draw the curtain and allow the scene to fade into the shadow of the past. That chapter is closed.

❖ Laura McMillan – Age 21
Seminary Ridge

I lived with my family on Seminary Ridge in our home called Wildwood when the American Civil War came to my town. My grandfather was among some of the first Scotch-Irish settlers in Adams County. My father, David, spent several years building our house here on the ridge and moved into it in 1841. He was a surveyor, a school teacher, and an orchardist. In fact, he planted a large orchard of apple, peach, plum, pear, and cherry trees when I was just a baby. He kept an account book listing all his trees, row by row.

I had an older brother named Oscar who volunteered for service and became a private in Company C of Cole's Maryland Cavalry. He served throughout the war, always furnishing his own horse to ride. In order to always have a fresh horse, he kept one or two of the animals here at home so they could rest from active service. In June of 1863 he came home on a short furlough to get a fresh horse. Returning to his unit he encountered a scouting party of Confederates in the southwest part of the county.

By the morning of July 1st everyone in Gettysburg knew a battle was imminent. When my father saw columns of Union soldiers coming up the Emmitsburg road toward the scene of the fighting west of town, he knew they would have to pass through our fields and orchards. So, he took his axe outside and chopped down our fences so the soldiers could move more quickly. Father followed the troops, even when they retreated to the Round Tops by the evening of the first day. He stayed there throughout the rest of the battle. When he was ordered to stay down flat behind the rocks for his own safety, he stayed on his knees, using the weapon of prayer. He besought his God for the victory for the cause to which he was devoted. When veterans returned to our town years after the battle they shared their memories of my aging father's earnest prayers as he shouted his petitions, kneeling upright behind the rocks of the Round Tops.

My sister Carrie was 18 years old in 1863. She and I carried buckets of water to fill the canteens of the soldiers as they ran by on the double-quick. While Carrie was down at the spring, which was about one quarter of a mile from the house, she became alarmed and ran across the field to the Bliss farm. She carried a small basket of clothes that she had planned to wash at the spring. As she passed some soldiers, she asked them to tell me where she was going. I could see her fleeing as I looked out a window. So, I quickly gathered up my father's Sunday suit, the family silver, and some other articles, then went to join Carrie. We met at the Bliss house, but again we were obliged to flee. Running across the fields, we came to the Weikert house at the back of Little Round Top. We stayed there, helping to bake bread and caring for the wounded.

It wasn't until July 8th that my father managed to go through the picket line and return to our home. He found it badly damaged, with nineteen cannon holes gaping in the walls and roof. A round bullet was imbedded in one of the doors, where it remains today. All of the furniture, books, bedding, clothing, surveying instruments and important papers from our house were entirely or partly buried under the quickly built earthworks that had been built to protect the cannons that were placed in our yard. The only piece of furniture left in the house was an eight-day mantle clock that was still running as it sat on a shelf above the fireplace. The floors were thick with mud since the heavy rains came in through the damaged roof. All of our crocks of apple butter were gone. (At the 75th anniversary of the battle a former Confederate soldier visited the cellar of our house where he said he had taken a crock of the most delicious apple butter he had ever tasted.) However, the Confederates left behind the tin cans of fruit we had been storing. Apparently they were not familiar with this new method of food preservation.

All of our cows, horses, chickens, turkeys, guineas and other livestock were gone. We were surprised to see one of our mother hens leading her little flock of newly hatched chicks as they looked for food. We worked with broom and hoe and shovel to rescue what we could, and then made a list of our property that was lost or destroyed. We girls worked hard at helping the family restore our beloved home "Wildwood".

This modern day view of the McMillan House shows the renovated and enlarged structure. In 1863 the home was surrounded by extensive orchards which are now being restored by the National Park Service.

❖ Sadie Hoffman – Age 6
Seminary Ridge (or perhaps the Chambersburg Pike!)

I was only six years old when the battle of Gettysburg was fought right on our farm located between Seminary Ridge and the Emmitsburg Road Since I was already an orphan I lived with my grandparents, Mr. and Mrs. Henry Spangler. I had spent the night at the neighbors, and when I was returning home on July 1st I saw soldiers running back and forth with field glasses. They shouted to me, "Run home, little girl. There's going to be a big battle!" I ran home as fast as I could to tell my grandparents, and they laughed at me. As my dear grandparents laughed in disbelief, tears came to my eyes.

Soon a Union soldier came for an ax to cut down the rail fences. He warned us, "Go to your cellars. Men are coming in strong on both sides." By this time Union soldiers were lying on the ground around the house. I helped my Aunt Sarah bake bread and pies as soldiers came into our house for food. They took the bread right off the heel and ate it as they ran.

A soldier in the doorway commanded us, "You must go to the cellar". Although Aunt Sarah wanted to finish her baking, Grandfather insisted that she join the rest of us downstairs. I remember it so clearly. We made ourselves quite comfortable since we had a good spring for water and most of our food was kept down there in the coolness. There were stools, benches, a workbench, and rows of crocks. On pegs near the outside cellar door hung horse bridles, a saddle and buggy harness. Although we were together and cozy inside, there was an awful conflict taking place outside in the yard. We could hear terrible screams of men and screams of cannon shells while we sat inside and prayed.

Grandfather prayed that the war would soon be over and that we would have one nation under God. Somehow, Aunt Sarah managed to churn the butter.

We stayed in the cellar until about 4:00. When we went upstairs we found ourselves between the Union and the Confederate lines. There were dead bodies lying on our porch. I just cried and cried. I was glad when Aunt Sarah asked me to help her work the bread dough into loaves. A Confederate officer came asking for the bread. He reminded his men, our enemy, that they must leave enough bread for our family. I liked that man, and that was why I started to cry again, a loud piteous wail. As Grandmother rocked me safe in her arms, I fell asleep. Grandfather helped by taking an armful of pillowcases and towels out to the doctors as they amputated arms and legs in our yard. He returned to get a scissors and a crock of lard to help keep the bandages from growing fast.

When we noticed our neighbor's house and my Uncle's barn on fire, we decided to try to save our moveable things. I saved my doll, her cradle, and my chair. As we were carrying furniture outside, Confederates were carrying their wounded inside. The men, beaten, dirty and silent, lay stacked on the floor like bags of wheat. A doctor asked Aunt Sarah for some homemade salve. Since she had to cross the room to reach it, she had to first take off her shoes, and then gently stepped on the bodies of the wounded. While in the kitchen she noticed the house was full of bullets and that a cannon ball had flown directly across the table where she had been standing to kneed the bread. Thank goodness Grandfather had insisted that she come to the cellar with us!

From the evening of the first day's battle until the end, we were in the Confederate line. On the second day of the battle we were too busy to stay in the cellar. Aunt Sarah continued baking. When they killed our chickens, Grandmother made soup. When I saw that they had killed my bantams, I did not cry. In fact, Grandmother had me laughing as we made "quick noodles" called rivels for our soup. We just had to add eggs and flour to the broth. I watched as Grandmother cared for a wounded soldier, and then placed him on a bench in the cellar, the only part of our home that was still at peace.

On the evening of July 2nd two Confederates asked to sleep in our kitchen. Aunt Sarah asked them, "How is the battle going?" The reply was "It's just this way – if General Lee doesn't give in we will have every man of us killed." On the third day they warned us that things would be getting worse. Grandfather refused to leave his house, but Grandmother, Sarah, and I walked west up to Seven Stars. Confederates were coming in steadily. Two soldiers helped us to the house of some friends. By evening, though, we decided it would be better to be together. So, we returned to the house with Grandfather. We found our barn had been set on fire after the Confederates took our hay.

The next day, Saturday, there was a thunderstorm, but it was not as loud as the battle. Then on Sunday wagons came to take the wounded away. I remember one soldier sitting at our kitchen table crying when they made him go. A few weeks later some Confederates came back to the house and told Sarah that they would never live in our house after the battle for fear of moans and groans and the dogs' howling. But Sarah said she had seen much worse and was not afraid. One day a gentleman came to the door and thanked Grandmother for saving his life. He insisted that she take some money, and we had a pleasant supper together.

There was much rainy weather after the battle. My grandfather used all the lime we had to disinfect the ground near our house. For years polite people would not talk about the battle in public. They would air out their house in the morning and close the windows at night. Every place was disinfected with lye, or turpentine. Every lady had a handkerchief edged in black lace, and mourning veils and mourning pins were worn. Married women wore black dresses and children and young ladies wore white. Every woman wore a ribbon or chain around her neck with a "smelling salts" bottle. Black umbrellas were used for rain and sun.

(This biography was created from a newspaper article featuring an interview with the subject Sarah (Sadie) Hoffman. However, research conducted by Timothy Smith and Elwood Christ of the Adams County Historical Society found records showing Sadie to be the granddaughter of Abraham and Elizabeth Spangler, not Mr. and Mrs. Henry Spangler. Her mother died shortly after Sadie was born and she was taken in by her grandparents (or perhaps someone she called her grandparents,) In 1863 her actual grandparents resided on a farm located on the Chambersburg Pike, the scene of the first day's battle, not the site she describes in her account. The details of her description certainly suggest she witnessed the Battle of Gettysburg. A "history mystery" does exist, however, awaiting further research and speculation!)

❧East of Town, and Two Out-of-Town Visitors

The following collection includes two civilians, plus a Union soldier from the area, a visitor from California, and a visitor from Kentucky! Lieutenant Isaac Durboraw represents one of over thirty local boys who had joined the Union Army and became members of the Pennsylvania Reserves, Company K. This unit is sometimes referred to as the "Boys who fought at home" since they were from the Gettysburg area *and* fought in the Battle of Gettysburg.

On July 2, 1863 the Pennsylvania Reserves stood strong against the Confederate charge through the Valley of Death along Plum Run, later nicknamed Bloody Run. Often John Burns, who was too old to join the Union army, is touted as the only civilian who fought the Rebels. Although the only civilian, he was certainly not the only local citizen who fought the Confederates by serving in the Union Army here and elsewhere throughout the war.

Likewise, Jennie Wade was not the only local citizen killed during the summer of 1863. William Washington Sandoe lived in Mount Joy Township near the church where his body is now buried. Although his death did not occur during the famous battles fought the first three days of July, he was killed by Confederates in late June as these enemy forces invaded Pennsylvania. His heartbreaking story is told by another local man, David Conover.

The account of James Tawney is of special interest since he was an eyewitness of the Cavalry battle fought east of town near his home on the Low Dutch Road. This battle was significant for several reasons including the fact Union Cavalry was able to hold against the more highly rated Confederate Cavalry. Additionally, George Armstrong Custer participated heroically leading the Michigan troops. Tawney was a Judge in Minnesota and his information was a part of a Memorial Day speech he presented here many years later.

The next civilian, a visitor, was included to emphasize the tenacity of the local citizens. Eliza Farnham should indeed be lauded for her dedicated assistance in the aftermath of the battle. Her account was taken from the diary she kept which was later published in a newspaper. One can sadly imagine the wealth of human interest stories that participants literally took to their graves. And, our final, and "first," citizen definitely has the most famous Gettysburg address!

This lovely wedding portrait shows George Washington Sandoe and his new bride. Today a marker stands on the Baltimore Pike near where he was killed on June 26, 1863, as Pennsylvania was invaded by Confederate forces. He was the first Union soldier to die at Gettysburg, and one of only two local citizens to die from enemy fire.

❖ James Tawney – Low Dutch Road

I was born in a house on the Low Dutch Road which connects the York Road and the Baltimore Pike. From its attic window my brother and I witnessed a memorable cavalry charge on the afternoon of July 3rd. We saw the gallant Union generals Custer and Gregg repulse and drive back the Confederate cavalry forces of J.E.B. Stuart and Fitzhugh Lee. What a sight to remember! And I remember how the roads radiated from the center of town like the spokes from the hub of a wheel. Their names will forever retain a precious old-world charm. There was a time that each of the farms, school houses and churches in the area were as familiar to me as its bed is to a brook. Whenever in imagination I linger over these scenes, a host of memories come trooping forth from every hill and wood land.

I remember exactly what I was doing on the morning of the opening day of the battle. I was high up in a big black cherry tree picking cherries for my mother. When I heard the first thundering tones of the battle roar over the countryside, I hastily climbed down out of that tree and ran home with my cherries. For a time our house was used as a hospital for the wounded. I remember the enemy commenced shelling it on July 3rd. It was saved only by the act of a Union soldier who unfurled my sister's red flannel petticoat from my fishing pole, which made a suitable flagstaff. This was placed on the highest chimney of the house and denoted our house as a hospital.

On the Tuesday after the battle I rode with my grandfather over the fields to Culp's Hill. There on the northern side of that hill I saw the bodies of some sixty soldiers lying in one uncovered grave. I can still hear the voices and see the faces of long ago as I wander through the woods and valleys. I remember like it was yesterday, listening to those immortal words from the lips of Abraham Lincoln as he uttered the dedication of the cemetery near the future site of the national monument. "Let us highly resolve that these honored dead shall not have died in vain." Would the American people make this resolve and keep it?

Forty- four years later, while living in Winona, Minnesota, I was asked to deliver the Memorial Day address near the exact same spot that President Lincoln spoke. I was introduced as "The Honorable James A. Tawney," and spoke to the usual throng of visitors from across the county and points beyond. The streets were lined with people as the annual procession started promptly at 1:30. I rode in a carriage behind the Citizen's Band and the Sons of Veterans Reserves. The second division of the parade was headed by the Gettysburg Drum Corps and included veterans on foot as well as in carriages. School children joined the parade at High Street. As we reached the cemetery the veterans and school children proceeded with the beautiful ceremony of strewing the graves with flowers while the band played a dirge. Next, the crowd gathered at the rostrum where the exercises began with a prayer.

Then, it was my turn to speak. What words could ever approximate a description of the awful scenes of those three days? What heart, no matter how large, could adequately appreciate the valor and enormous cost of that fight for the Nation's life? I told the crowd that it was more important for them to think about and appreciate the heritage of glory from which we come than for them to hear me describe what I remember. "In silence, beneath these skies, where everyone can be alone with God, it is fitting that we take to heart the lessons of these graves, hills, and fields."

❖ Isaac Durboraw, Lt. in Co. K, 30th PA
Age 22 – Two Taverns on Baltimore Pike

Who would have ever thought that I would be marching with the Union army, enroute to fight the Confederates, so close to my own home near Gettysburg? Not only did I see familiar scenes along the way, but I also recognized many faces. When I called out the names of girls as they stood waving their handkerchiefs at us, they stared in amazement. It seems they did not recognize me. Actually, our Sergeant Young marched right by his home and was greeted by his brother. But the sergeant did not leave the ranks.

Just before noon on July 2nd we bivouacked along the Baltimore Pike in J.M. Diehl's field, got some rest and waited for orders. While cooking coffee I was told that Peter Baker, who lived nearby, wanted to see me. I went to the Baker house, had something to eat, and returned promptly to the company. As I reached the command, orders were given to fall in double quick. Immediately we were ordered to advance to the Round Tops. We obliqued into position, and when the command "Forward" was given, every man had to hunt his way the best that he could. We ventured over, around, and through bushes, rocks, stones, and finally Plum Run swamp. There we ran smack into the Rebels and forced them back. When we got to the Wheatfield, our line was halted and established at a stone fence.

Later I told Captain Minnigh that I was going home and he should neither say yes or no. I went back to where we had piled our knapsacks the day before, but could find neither my knapsack nor the guard. Eventually I found it in a quarry on the banks of Rock Creek. Since my home was only three miles away I reached it quickly. It was filled with wounded soldiers, including

Union General Meredith. I had to sleep on the floor, but I was able to fill my knapsack before returning to my company the next morning. I noticed that most of my neighbors had left the area, and now their homes were filled with skulkers and shuysters absent from their commands. When I finally got back to my company I shared the contents of my haversack. When we marched that night, my haversack was empty.

Today on the south-west quadrant of Lincoln Square stands a memorial to Company K, the Boys Who Fought At Home. It serves as a reminder of Durboraw and other local men who had joined the Union Army and fought in the Battle of Gettysburg. He was later injured when someone dropped a cannonball on his foot. He died in 1895 from a fall off of a barn he was helping to take down, a casualty of work in a time of peace.

❖ David Conover – Age 18
Baltimore Pike

I was eighteen at the time of the three- day battle in July. However, my biggest memory of the Rebel raid was on Friday, June 26th, the day that the first soldier was killed at Gettysburg. For months there had been Rebel raids and rumors, and with each scare we would take our horses to a safer place. This time I told my mother that I was not running until I actually saw some Rebels. Well, on that particular day I went up to the Diamond of the town with a party of young men from my neighborhood. While there I first heard the news that the Rebs were coming. As we walked down Chambersburg Street there was a great commotion at the Eagle Hotel. Philadelphia troops and other cavalry soldiers were there. A city trooper came out of the hotel, and finding his horse gone, jumped on a horse without a saddle. Then he and his unit skedaddled as fast as they could go out the York Pike.

Our crowd went on out to Seminary Ridge to take a look. As the Rebels came in sight, our people ran off in all directions! My friends and I turned and ran even before we saw the Rebels. As we ran back up Baltimore Street we heard shooting on the Diamond, and by the time we reached the Cemetery Gate House, Confederates overtook us. An enemy soldier shot his pistol for us to stop, and asked if we were soldiers or citizens. When we replied that we were citizens, he warned us to never run away from the enemy or we might be shot. He said, "If you hadn't stopped I would have killed one of you, and I wouldn't have done that for all the states."

We were sent back down to the center of town. As we walked back by the cemetery, Mrs. Thorn, the wife of the caretaker, and her mother were both weeping. Our Rebel captor insisted it was entirely our fault that the women were frightened and crying. And again, he reminded us never to run. Matilda Pierce and her sister were crying wonderfully about the loss of their beloved horse that had been taken by the Rebels. (I guess that wasn't our fault!)

We were in the Diamond only a short time when Early's Rebel infantry arrived, boasting that they were on their way to Philadelphia and Washington. When our spirits returned we told those Rebs they had their biggest undertaking ahead of them if they tried that. When the Confederates asked to see the town authorities to demand money, citizens answered that they had gone and taken all the funds. When they were told that the only way they could get money was by pressing the citizens, the Confederate replied that they wouldn't do that.

Two boyish looking Rebel soldiers inquired about some of the leading citizens and college professors. It seems that they had formerly been students at our Pennsylvania College, and they were given the requested information. Actually, the rank and file of the Rebel army was much more intelligent than I had expected. As I spoke with some of them I found no depredations or improper behavior. They were actually quite peaceable. At about five o'clock we wanted to go home so we asked an officer for a pass. He wrote a note on a piece of paper that he held up against the wall of Spangler's store.

Even with a pass, we certainly did not feel it was safe enough to go out the main road. So, we decided to go out past the

Reformed Church, around Culp's Hill, and on to McAllister's Mill. As we were leaving town I saw a Rebel cavalryman leading a horse, saying, "Here is the horse. I've shot the rider. I am sorry, but I had to do it in self defense." As we traveled we came upon a whole flat covered with Rebels. We safely made our way through the woods. But upon reaching the McAllister place I heard that a man had been killed in his fields along the Baltimore Pike. He was identified by the neighbors as George Washington Sandoe from Mount Joy Township, down the Taneytown Road below the church. He had recently joined Bell's Cavalry of Home Guard, was carrying a pistol but not wearing a uniform. My mother told me that young Mr. Lightner had come to our house earlier and told her that he and Sandoe were riding along Rock Creek on their way home when they saw Rebs coming their way. As they urged their horses on, his horse took a fence, but Sandoe's horse refused. Lightner rode on. Hearing gunfire, he feared his comrade had been shot. Sandoe's body was later found in a field near the road. I guess that was his horse I had seen being led down Baltimore Street as I was leaving town.

That night I tied our horses in the bushes along the creek, but the next morning, when I found the pike clear, I put them back in the stable where they belonged.

❖ Eliza Farnham – Age 47
Visitor from California

Many of my friends in California knew me as the first public school teacher of the spiritual philosophy and the rights of women. Although I was well-suited to the duties of a nurse at the bedside of a friend, I was not able to endure the fatigue of serving hundreds of sufferers. I happened to be lecturing in Philadelphia for the Spiritualist Society on Saturday July 4th when the news of the great battle arrived.

I was determined to go to Gettysburg and do what I could. I got a cheap calico and made it up in a few hours, with a little help. Then at midnight, after my lecture, I left for this place with three other women. We traveled via Baltimore and had a battle there, with the red tape department. We finally arrived in Gettysburg on July 6th at six in the evening.

On July 7th we breakfasted at six then went across the street to the Lutheran church which was serving as a hospital. In fact, the whole town was one vast hospital. All public and a great many private buildings were full of sufferers. All states from health to death were before us! We traveled by field ambulance to the field hospitals on the battle ground.

It is impossible to describe in a letter what we saw on that drive. Although the human dead were removed from the road by then, there were horses strewn along much of the way. The earth of the roads as well as the fields was ploughed to mire by the army wheels and horses. Straggling wounded still lined the roads and rested against any fences that were not torn down or burnt up.

~ 111 ~

Breastworks, ground piled up to protect artillery positions, loomed up here and there in the desolate fields.

We left the road to cross a trampled meadow toward a wooded height. As we went there we could see cities of tents on all hands. These were the field hospitals of the different corps that had engaged in this frightful battle. When we reached the place we were bound for there appeared before us avenues of white tents under the green boughs. Oh, but what those quiet-looking tents held! It is absolutely inconceivable, unless you actually see it, what spectacles awaited us on the slopes of the hills around us.

There were miles of tents and acres of men lying on the open earth beneath the trees. I could never have imagined anything to compare to this. There were dead, and dying, and wounded in every condition you can imagine. This was the result of two (actually three) days of such a horrible rain of missiles. Old veterans who had seen all our battles said they had never seen such firing anywhere.

I worked from ten until half past four spreading, cutting and distributing bread and butter without five minutes cessation. Such thankful eyes and stifled voices came from those poor wounded fellows who were left without legs, or arms, or hands. Many had eaten nothing but hardtack since they were hurt. I had the pleasure of giving a piece of bread and butter to Colonel Fry of Sacramento. Although shot in the ankle, he seems well and very resolute. Beside him lay a man and his son, each having lost a leg. Some men had both legs gone. It was even more horrible, though, to see the awful pile of these limbs piled at the foot of a tree in front of the surgeons' tent.

I tried to keep my friends in California informed of my work, but the work was just too exhausting. Some say that I sacrificed my life to my sense of duty to these suffering countrymen on the field of battle. I could not endure the fatigue of serving hundreds of sufferers, all the while feeling a constant inability to give adequate relief. Although I stayed in Gettysburg only four days, it is said I left bearing the seeds of death. For a long time I could not sleep. Then, after six months of suffering, I died. At the time it was reported that I died of consumption. But that is not true. Instead, my death was caused by the simple loss of vitality caused by the drain on my system at Gettysburg.

Eliza Farnham was a 19th-century novelist, feminist, abolitionist, novelist, and activist for prison reform. She died of consumption in New York City.

❖ Abraham Lincoln – Age 54
Gettysburg Address – 719 Baltimore Street

The Soldiers' National Cemetery- what he dedicated *or* 799 Baltimore Street – The Evergreen Cemetery – where he stood to deliver his speech

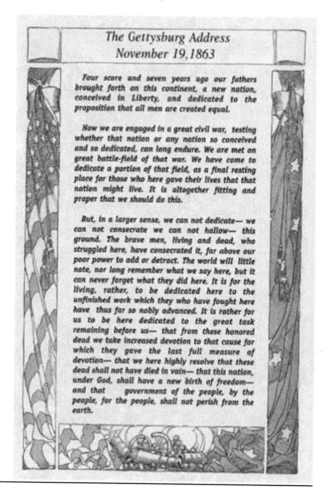

The Gettysburg Address
November 19, 1863

Four score and seven years ago our fathers brought forth on this continent, a new nation, conceived in Liberty, and dedicated to the proposition that all men are created equal.

Now we are engaged in a great civil war, testing whether that nation or any nation so conceived and so dedicated, can long endure. We are met on great battle-field of that war. We have come to dedicate a portion of that field, as a final resting place for those who here gave their lives that that nation might live. It is altogether fitting and proper that we should do this.

But, in a larger sense, we can not dedicate— we can not consecrate we can not hallow— this ground. The brave men, living and dead, who struggled here, have consecrated it, far above our poor power to add or detract. The world will little note, nor long remember what we say here, but it can never forget what they did here. It is for the living, rather, to be dedicated here to the unfinished work which they who have fought here have thus far so nobly advanced. It is rather for us to be here dedicated to the great task remaining before us— that from these honored dead we take increased devotion to that cause for which they gave the last full measure of devotion— that we here highly resolve that these dead shall not have died in vain— that this nation, under God, shall have a new birth of freedom— and that government of the people, by the people, for the people, shall not perish from the earth.

❧Bibliography of Sources

The following files are available at the Adams County Historical Society located on Seminary Ridge in Gettysburg, Pennsylvania

★ Auchinbaugh, Nellie information from "Nellie Auchinbaugh: Personal Experiences"
★ Barr, Agnes information from her personal memoirs, written perhaps around the 25th anniversary of the battle in 1888, or as late as 1904 when Theodore Roosevelt came to town, or 1909 when President Taft came to dedicate the U.S. Regular's Monument of the battlefield.
★ Bayly, Harriet information from "Mrs. Bayly's Battle Story"
★ Bayly, William information from "Memoir of a Thirteen-year-old Boy Relating to the Battle of Gettysburg"
★ Broadhead, Sarah information from "A Diary of a Lady of Gettysburg, Pennsylvania from June 15 to July 15, 1863," currently published by Gary Hawbaker, Hershey, PA
★ Buehler, Fannie and David information from "Recollections of the Rebel Invasion and One Woman's Experience During the Battle of Gettysburg," by Fannie Buehler written at the request of her children in 1896. Reprinted by Gary Hawbaker, Hershey, PA 2002
★ Burns, John information from newspaper article "the Civilian Hero of Gettysburg" which appeared in the Gettysburg Times 75th Anniversary Edition, July 1938.
★ Conover, David information from newspaper article entitled "The Killing of Geo. W. Sandoe: A Battle Story Told By David A. Conover" published in the Gettysburg Compiler, September, 1905 (On file at the ACHS)
★ Durboraw, Isaac information from first-hand account on file at ACHS

- ★ Farnham, Eliza information from an article entitled "Eliza Farnham: Description of Scenes After the Battle of Gettysburg" published in Common Sense, August, 22, 1874

- ★ Gilbert, Elizabeth information taken from a document written by her granddaughter, Olivia Gilbert Gillan and transcribed by the Adams County Historical Society by Elsie Singmaster Lewars

- ★ Harman, Amelia information from "Burning of the M'Lean Home on the First Day's Battle of Gettysburg" Gettysburg Compiler, July 15, 1915

- ★ Hoffman, Sadie information from newspaper article entitled "Miss Sadie Hoffman Remembers Gettysburg" by Mary K. Dissinger

- ★ Jacobs, Henry and Julia information from "How an Eyewitness Watched the Great Battle," published in the Baltimore American Newspaper, June 20, 1918 McAllister, Mary information from an article in the Philadelphia Inquier dated June 1938

- ★ King, Sarah Barrett "A Mother's Story"

- ★ McClellan, Georgia information from: The Jennie Wade Story: A True and Complete Account of the Only civilian Killed During the Battle of Gettysburg, by Cindy L. Small, published by Thomas Publications, Gettysburg, 1991

- ★ McMillan, Laura information from GNMP file: a historical document recorded by Margaret McMillan, granddaughter of David McMillan, January 6, 1941.

- ★ Pierce, Matilda information from At Gettysburg, What a Girl Saw and Heard of the Battle, by Tillie Pierce Alleman, 1889. Reprinted by Butternut and Blue, Baltimore, Maryland, 1987.

- ★ Schick, Charles information from an article entitled "Chicagoan Describes Battle He Witnessed as Boy of 7". Published in the 75th Anniversary of the Gettysburg Times, July 1938 (Taken from an article published in a Chicago newspaper, then sent to someone in Gettysburg who submitted it to the local newspaper)

- ★ Shuey, T.F. information from "How Battle of Gettysburg Impressed college Student" published in The National

Republican, Washington, D.C., 1869, which includes his actual diary accounts

★ Skelly, Annie information from a recollection she signed and affirmed on December 8, 1941.(On file at ACHS)

★ Skelly, Daniel information from A Boy's Experience During the Battle of Gettysburg, self-published in Gettysburg 1932.

★ Thorn, Elizabeth information from "A Woman's Thrilling Experiences of the Battle" by Elizabeth Thorn, published in the Gettysburg Compiler, July 26, 1903

★ Warren, Mary information from "Memories of the Battle" by Mary Warren Fastnacht, York, Pennsylvania, 1928

★ Yount (Stumph), Emma information from a letter she wrote to your son in 1943.

★ Ziegler (Clare), Lydia information taken from a manuscript she wrote around 1900 entitled "A Girl's Story of the Great Battle"

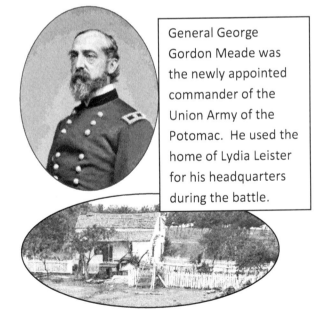

General George Gordon Meade was the newly appointed commander of the Union Army of the Potomac. He used the home of Lydia Leister for his headquarters during the battle.

❧Books

★ Bennett, Gerald R. "Days of Uncertainty and Dread": The Ordeal Endured by the Citizens at Gettysburg. Gettysburg, PA: Gerald Bennett R., 1994. – This is an excellent source of information about the houses and families living in Gettysburg at the time of the battle.

★ Frassanito, William A. Early Photography at Gettysburg Gettysburg, PA: Thomas Publications, 1995 – This book is about more than photography! Much knowledge about the citizens of 1863 citizens of Gettysburg is revealed in the text.

★ Kennell, Brian, A Beyond the Gatehouse: Gettysburg's Evergreen Cemetery Gettysburg, PA: Evergreen Cemetery Association, 2000.-This excellent book includes a history of the civilian cemetery as well as noted "residents."

★ Petruzzi, J. David. The Complete Gettysburg Guide.- Walking and Drivin g Tours of the Battlefield, Town, Cemeteries, Field Hospital Sites, and other Topics of Historical Interest New York: Savas Beatie, 2009 – The subtitle tells it all, complete with ample maps and photographs.

★ Slade, Jim and Alexander, John. Firestorm at Gettysburg: Civilian Voices Atglen, PA: Schiffer Military/Aviation History, 1998 - As the title suggests, quotations from 1863 citizens are arranged chronologically amidst photography.

❧Websites

✪ www.achs.pa.org – The Adams County Historical Society website serves as a key to what information is available at their new facility.

✪ www.gettysburg.stonesentinels.com – Stone Sentinels is a comprehensive source of monument images and information for the over 1,200 located on the Gettysburg Battlefield today.

✪ www.gettysburgdaily.com – As the name implies, Gettysburg Daily is an excellent source of Gettysburg information on a daily basis. The editor/creator is a Licensed Battlefield Guide and the site often includes videos of LBG presentations on topics of interest. Current events are covered as well as historical interpretation.

✪ www.loc.gov. – The Library of Congress website is a truly remarkable source of information and images. The American Memory Pages and Digital Collections are outstanding resources on many historical topics.

✪ www.nps.gov/gett/index.htm - The National Park Service site for Gettysburg National Military Park contains a wealth of information on the Gettysburg, the Battlefield, and touring the area.

❧Image Credits

1. Map of Gettysburg – Original map by LMC

2. Map - Theodore Ditterline. *Ditterline Map*. 1863. Map. www.memory.loc.com, Washington, D.C. Web. 3 Mar 2012

3. Ron Tunnsion. *Elizabeth Thorn*. 2002. Sculpture. www.evergreencemetery.org, Gettysburg, PA. Web. 3 Mar 2012.

4. -----*Baltimore Street 1863*. Photograph. http://passionforthepast.blogspot.com. Web. 3 Mar 2012

5. Bronze plaque – Original photograph by LMC

6. ---- *Gettysburg 1857 Public School*. www.kevintrostle.com. Gettysburg, PA Web. 3 Mar 2012

7. ---- *Matilda Pierce*. Photograph www.jennie-wade-house.com. Web. 3 Mar 2012

8. ----*Weikert House*. Photograph.

9. ---*Wade Sisters* - http://july1863.homestead.com. Web. 3 Mar 2012

10. ---*McClellan House* http://july1863.homestead.com

11. --- *Peter and Elizabeth Thorn*. Photograph. .www.evergreencemetery.org

12. ---*Gatehouse* – Photograph. www.evergreencemetery.org. Gettysburg, PA Web, 3 Mar 2012

13. Brady & Co. *John L. Burns, the old hero of Gettysburg*. 1863. Photograph. www.memory.loc.gov. Washington, D.C. Web. 3 Mar 2012

14. ----*Christ Lutheran Church*. Photograph. www.gettysburgdaily.com Web. 3 Mar 2012

15. ----*Open-book statue*. Photograph. www.gettysburgdaily.com Web. 3 Mar 2012

16. ----- *Eagle Hotel, Chambersburg Street*. Photograph. www.gettysburgdaily.com Web. 3 Mar 2012

17. ----*Thompson House (Lee's Headquarters)*. Photograph. www.gettysburgdaily.com Web. 3 Mar 2012

18. ----*General Robert E. Lee*. Photograph. www.wikipedia.org Web. 3 Mar 2012

19. ----*Sarah Broadhead*. Photograph. www.pacivilwar150.com Web. 2 Mar 2012

20. ----*John Burns Statue*. Statue. www.americasbesthistory.com Web. 2 Mar 2012

21. Brady & Co. *John L. Burns, the old hero of Gettysburg*. 1863. Photograph. www.memory.loc.gov. Washington, D.C. Web. 3 Mar 2012

22. Gardner and Co. *Fahnestock Building*.1863. Photograph. www.gettysburgdaily.com Gettysburg, PA Web. 3 Mar 2012

23. ----- *Lincoln's Gettysburg Address,* Gettysburg. Photograph. 1863 Nov.19. www.loc.gov 3 Mar 2012

24. Mumper & Co. *Confederate Dead Gathered at Gettysburg.* 1863. Photograph. www.memory.loc.com. Washington, D.C. Web. 3 Mar 2012

25. O'Sullivan, Timothy. *A Harvest of Death.* 1863. Photograph. www.memory.loc.com. Washington, D. C. Web. 3 Mar 2012

26. ----*Henry Eyster Jacobs.* Photograph. www.gettysburgdaily.com Web. 3 Mar 2012

27. ----*Daniel Skelly.* Photograph. www.thomaslegion.net. Web. 3 Mar 2012

28. Waud, Alfred. *Death of Reynolds-Gettysburg.*1863. Drawing.www.loc.gov. Washington, D.C. Web. 3 Mar 2012

29. ----*Gettysburg(View from West).* Photograph – www.nps.gov. Web. 3 Mar 2012

30. ----*McMillan House* www.gettysburgdaily.com. Web 3 Mar 2012

31. ----*Henry Spangler House.* Photograph. www.loc.gov Web. 3 Mar 2012

32. ----*Mr. and Mrs. George Sandoe.* Photograph. www.gettysburgdaily.com. Web. 3 Mar 2012

33. ----*Company K Memorial.* Photograph. www.gettysburg.stonesentinels.com Web. 3 Mar 2012

34. ----*Isaac Durboraw.* Photograph. www.findagrave.com Web. 3 Mar 2012

35. ----*Eliza Farnham.* Photograph. www.historichwy49.com/women Web. 3 Mar 2012

36. ----*Lincoln's Gettysburg Address*

37. Gardner, Alexander. *General Meade's Headquarters at Gettysburg.*1863. Photograph. Memory.loc.com. Washington, D.C. Web. 3 Mar 2012

38. Tyson Brothers. *Lydia Ziegler* Photograph. www.geneologystories.net Web. 3 Mar 2012

39. ----- *Peter and Elizabeth Thorn.* Photograph. www.evergreencemetery.org Web. 3 Mar 2012

40. Tipton Brothers, Lydia Catherine Ziegler. Photograph. www.geneologystories.net Web, 3 Mar 2012

Notes~

Other Books by the Author:

📖 Star Light, Star Bright: A Tale of Old Gettysburg

Mary Matilda Mickley loves going to school and writing poetry, but she sorely misses her dear mother and her recently married sister. The summer of 1863 finds the American Civil War being fought right through Mary's town, and she learns more in a season than in a lifetime.

The book presents the actual experiences of real 1863 citizens of Gettysburg through young Mary's eyes. The story intertwines original *poetry* and *literary selections* taken from an actual reading textbook of the period to provide today's readers a glimpse of the education of yesterday. Come face to face with some of the real citizens of Gettysburg who had front row seats to history in the making, and President Lincoln's most famous speech.

Real 1863 citizens featured in the book include Mary Virginia Wade, Matilda Pierce, Rebecca Eyster, Amelia Harman, Elizabeth Thorn, Georgia McClellan, Wesley Culp, David Kendlehart, Hugh Scott, *and* President Abraham Lincoln and First Lady Mary Todd Lincoln.

Check out the easy-to-use online Learning Guide available for this book at www.pausetoreadbooks.webs.com

Meet the Author: As a native of Gettysburg Linda Clark found her passion for books and the Civil War through a juvenile fiction book presented by her third grade teacher at Eisenhower Elementary School. Now a retired school librarian and an emeritus Licensed Battlefield Guide, she enjoys researching the citizens of her hometown and telling their personal stories of the Battle of Gettysburg. Hopefully these people of the past will inspire readers today. She and her husband have a Gettysburg address with a view of the sun setting over the Blue Ridge,

Nonfiction Series by the Author:

📖 **The Battle For Gettysburg:** **What Was It Like For the Citizens of 1863?**

📖 **The Battle For Gettysburg – Two's:** **What Was It Like For the Citizens of 1863?**

📖 **The Battle For Gettysburg – 3:** **Close Calls, Near Misses, and Tragic Hits**

📖 **The Battle For Gettysburg – 4: Walk A Mile With Lincoln**

View the Battle of Gettysburg and its aftermath through the eyes of an array of real local citizens who witnessed this human tragedy of catastrophic proportion. Relive the horrific experiences of Elizabeth Thorn, John Burns, Sarah Broadhead, Matilda Pierce, Lydia Ziegler, Fannie Buehler, Georgia McClellan, Laura McMillan, and others. Biographical sketches are arranged by their Gettysburg addresses.

Extracted from first-hand accounts and other reference sources, these distillations of remembrances are certain to enlighten the mind and inspire the spirit.

The fifth book in the *Battle For Gettysburg Series* is entitled:

📖 Wounded Houses ~ Shattered Lives.

It features 30 structures that played a role in the battle of Gettysburg. Although the actual citizens of 1863 are no longer with us, their dwellings remain as reminders of their heroic stories of bravery. Bullet holes and cannon shells are still visible in some of the walls! The houses in the book are arranged along an 18-mile-long "tour route" that can be followed to view the structures.

These books are available at select bookstores and gift shops in the Gettysburg area. Or, for information on ordering additional copies visit the website:

www.pausetoreadbooks.webs.com

For additional information, email directly to:

pausetoread@yahoo.com

Thanks for pausing to read!

The following excerpt is taken directly from the account of Lydia Catherine Ziegler who was thirteen years old when she witnessed the Battle of Gettysburg. It was apparently told orally to a stenographer around 1900. This and similar primary sources were utilized in the creation of this book.

"After listening to the pitiful story told us of losing four sons in the war, and knowing their last son had been in the battle of Gettysburg, and walking all of the twenty-one miles over the mountains from Chambersburg, since there was no other mode of travel for them, and carrying all this distance a satchel filled with dainties such as Charlie was fond of, we attempted to help them. And their son Charlie was found lying in one of the rooms of the third floor of the Seminary building in a dying condition. The cries of that mother as she bent over the body of her boy were heartbreaking. For a short time consciousness returned to Charlie, and he knew his parents, who shortly after had at least some measure of comfort in taking his dead body home for burial.

I should like to tell you more about my varied experiences during the three months our home was used as a hospital, but my story has already become too lengthy."

~ Lydia Catherine Ziegler

Acknowledgments

I will always be indebted to the people who have made this novel possible.

My mum, Pam, and my stronger half, Nicola, whose initial reaction, ideas and notes on my work I trust implicitly. Carole Kendal for her meticulous proofreading. My designer Stuart Bache for yet another incredible cover design. My superb agent, Millie Hoskins at United Agents, and Dave Gaughran for his invaluable support and advice. And Keira Bowie for her ongoing patience and help.

Milton Keynes UK
Ingram Content Group UK Ltd.
UKHW022138060624
443846UK00033BB/502